A Vision

Not a Blueprint

A Vision

Not a Blueprint

Weldon Wyatt and Sage Valley

CURT SAMPSON

Additional information contact:

Sage Valley Golf Club

2240 Sage Valley Dr.

Graniteville, SC 29829

Book/cover design: Suzanna Brown O! Suzanna

www.osuzanna.com

ISBN 978-0-9801216-0-5

Printed in the United States of America

For my first editor, my mother, Ann.

CONTENTS

INTRODUCTION

*S*age Valley Golf Club dozes in a vast pine thicket so dense and quiet you can lose track of what country you're in. No highway noise disturbs the muted swish of wind through the trees and the hoot and coo of unseen birds. The unchanging soundtrack is punctuated at sunrise by the high whir of leaf blowers and at twilight by a bagpipe version of "Amazing Grace." A tape of the ancient Scottish hymn booms from six speakers mounted on the clubhouse roof. You can be over in the hunting preserve, more than a mile away, and still hear it. It always casts a spell. You can't help but stop what you're doing and sing along: "wa-as blind/ but now/I see."

This ritual gets very quickly to the point of the man who built the place.

The words to "Amazing Grace" come from Chronicles, chapter seventeen, in which King David marvels at God's choosing him and his house. That's Weldon Eugene Wyatt all over. The founder and hands-on owner of Sage Valley feels very strongly that his entrepreneurial genius was a gift from above, so the wealth that comes to him as naturally as breath is not his own. Therefore he has no problem giving money—*a lot* of money—to churches, schools, junior golf, environmental protection, and a South Carolina literacy program called Dollars for Scholars. His only problem with philanthropy is that it sometimes causes his face and name to wind up in the newspaper. He hates that.

"It says a lot that he's so private about his charity," says Ashley Wyatt Donaldson, his middle child. "A lot of people want a pat on the back. He doesn't need the approval."

Faith explains Wyatt's "drive to do good," as his wife Brenda calls it—and his belief in perfection, as expressed in the golf and bird-hunting heaven of Sage Valley. But religion is by no means the only thing propelling him; a lot of trends and history are contained within this one man. The Depression had ended when he was born, but when you observe habits such as Wyatt's insistence that every fallen pine in the 9000-acre Sage Valley forest gets trimmed and used for *something*, it's plain that he absorbed the waste-not lessons of a previous generation. Small town South Carolina is a less tangible element of his personality, but it's there; he's lived all his life in the triangle-shaped state, and embodies a lot of its quirks and pride. The rise of big-box retailers in the United States shaped his fortune and the savings-and-loan scandal made it—temporarily—vanish. His parents made him what he is to a degree—"I got my entrepreneurial drive from my dad and my attention to detail, and my neat freak, from my mom," he says—but Brenda enabled his success and his three children inspired it.

At least two other institutions affected Weldon Wyatt deeply. The thirteen-week United States Marine Corps boot camp, the toughest military training in the world, had a profound and permanent impact on his life. It's one source of his focus, his discipline, and his deep understanding of how a team can work—with him as the leader.

Myth surrounds Wyatt's relationship with a final organization, Augusta National Golf Club. Perhaps the legend lives because Sage Valley resides just a twenty-minute drive from the home of the Masters. They look alike: the two courses on either side of the Savannah River were designed by master architects on nearly identical terrain overlooked by virtually identical long leafs and loblollies. Both are very private and very focused on golf and great food. Neither golf course is a mere "amenity"—odious word—to enable the sale of residential lots. So at neither club will you observe wet or sweaty swimmers or red-faced tennis ball bashers or soccer moms in SUVs. Still, the proximity and similarity of these two courses are enough for some gathered in various Georgialina nineteenth holes to tell you that Weldon Wyatt founded Sage Valley because he was not invited to join Augusta National.

It's not true. And it's not the only fable obscuring the man. Some people state—once this anecdote was even published—that Weldon and his brother Joe drove fourteen hours to Bentonville, Arkansas in the early '80s, uninvited and without an appointment, to sit and pace in the Wal-Mart headquarters waiting room *all day* before Sam Walton himself came out to talk to them about building a store in Aiken. One version has him waiting around for two weeks. Again, a canard.

"I've heard so many stories about myself that when I hear stories about anyone in the public eye—about say, Warren Buffett—I wonder how much fact there is there," Wyatt says.

Probably the invented bits of history arose because Sage Valley Golf Club was such an instant hit upon its debut in 2001, making various Top One Hundred lists with unprecedented speed. The contiguous Sage Valley Hunt Club rose to world renown just as quickly. So who built this gem, people wanted to know, and how and why? But there were no answers. Wyatt had never been interested in talking about himself, and he didn't start now that he had a famous playground.

——-HOW WOULD THEY KNOW HE HAD A MIND SO AGILE? PERHAPS IF THEY'D TAUGHT ALGEBRA AND SOCIAL STUDIES SIMULTANEOUSLY, HIS ABILITY TO KEEP TRACK WOULD HAVE REVEALED ITSELF——-

Newspapers files and magazine profiles of Weldon Wyatt simply did not exist, and the idea of a Wyatt Development spokesperson or publicist churning out press releases is ludicrous. He reminds you of Robert Woodard, the brilliant CEO of Coca-Cola, who paid a man to keep his name *out* of the press.

But now at age sixty-eight Wyatt desires to explain his life and times to his children and to his children's children. His biographer—me—worried about his reticence. After a lifetime of reading people, of being an observer and not the observed, would he, I wondered, squirm and sigh and look out the window under questioning? He did not. Although he is not in love with the sound of his own voice or his own cleverness, and occasionally his darting eyes betrayed a trapped feeling, Wyatt listened to questions carefully and responded thoughtfully. But when the questions were vague or from deep left field, he formed his mouth into an O and knit his brows. I saw the O and the squint the day I told him that he and Donald Trump were in many ways quite alike, and when I pointed out his similarities to Willie Nelson.

We met at Sage Valley in April 2007, and again in May, July, and September. I visited the towns where he lived, and his church, and Parris Island. I spoke with business associates, his managers at Sage Valley (he hires the best), his wife, his daughter, his sister, his son, his secretary, and a teammate on the 1955 Chesnee Eagles basketball team. I came to know an intriguing man. Several intimates stated plainly that he is not a patient person—the word *antsy* came up several times—while another says, on the contrary, he is a *very* patient man. Obviously, he is both. He travels but doesn't fly; he's got one of those giant buses, like the ones Davis Love and John Daly use to follow the PGA Tour (his son Tom borrows it to tailgate—very stylishly—at University of South Carolina football games). He quotes the Bible and his father about equally. Dozens of golf titles line the bookcase in his office, including histories of the best clubs: Pine Valley, Oakmont, Riviera, Royal St. George's. He's got Churchill's five-book history of World War II, *The Annals of America* (twenty-one volumes), and *Words and Phrases* (fifty volumes). He is religious without being pious. His one vice—now abandoned—was card playing. Wyatt doesn't care for vacations, or cocktail hour, or going out to dinner. "I'm not social," he says, although people fascinate him, and he used to throw an annual party that invited guests planned their schedules around. He's made great food and wine a hallmark of Sage Valley but his own taste runs to cornbread, coleslaw, and iced tea. He's a student and admirer of the way Augusta National founders Bobby Jones and Clifford Roberts operated their club. Doesn't have a computer—"I wouldn't know how to turn one on." Abhors cell phones and doesn't allow their use at Sage Valley, except behind closed doors. Education is one of his great causes, yet his own grades were deplorable; he quit Graniteville High well short of graduation. South Carolina public schools simply had no way of measuring his kind of intelligence.

But then how would they ever know that the bored boy in the back of the classroom had a mind so agile? Perhaps if they'd taught Algebra and Geography and Social Studies simultaneously, then his ability to keep track would have revealed itself. While discussing the sequence of his life in the '80s, Wyatt casually mentioned that he "got foolin' with some restaurants." Define "foolin," his visitor requested. Define "some." He did: at the same time Wyatt Development Company's shopping-center construction business was taking off—with the intricacies and headaches that implies—Wyatt built and operated *nine* franchises of the Duff's Smorgasbord chain. With menus, health inspectors, portion control, dishwashers, advertising, and the price of noodles, all multiplied by nine—and still with his baseline preoccupations from the development company—how could he sleep at night?

He shrugged. "I've always been able to delegate," he said.

Sage Valley Golf Club General Manager Dave Christensen puts it this way: "When Weldon gives you a project, he wants you on it right *now*. He tells you what he wants but not how to do it. He said to me, 'Dave, we're gonna buy another 8000 acres. We'll put a hunting preserve on it, with a pine-log lodge with world class hunting dogs and mule-drawn wagons. In five years, I want us to be known as much for quail hunting as for golf.' Before that it was, "I want a private golf course with elevation change, moving water, uncut timber, and close to a major airport and an Interstate.' Then it was 'I want a clubhouse that can seat 200, with big shower heads in the locker room and in the cabins, and excellent food.' He wants you to go to bed dreaming about how to make things first-class. He has a vision, not a blueprint."

Wyatt's vision for himself does not seem to include a lot of downtime. But since he believes that a round of golf reveals character more quickly and with more clarity than just about anything else, I should report on our half a round together: We played at breakneck speed, finishing nine holes in ninety minutes. We had a cart *and* caddies—the owner of Sage Valley likes to walk downhill and ride uphill. He spoke on his walkie-talkie on almost every hole, most often with his superintendent, Chuck Green. He told a few brief anecdotes about the course, including something the architect said before the bulldozers roared: "We were in a meeting, and someone asked me how I got Fazio. Fazio said, 'I'll answer that. I asked Weldon how many memberships he needed to sell right away and he said, "none." I asked him how many houses he'd have to have on the golf course and he said "none." So I said, "when do we start?'"

Wyatt's a pretty good but out-of-practice golfer—his back swing breaks down at the top and his grip is a little off, particularly the right thumb—but he was consistently in the fairway off the tee. His putter is a Frank Johnston Original, circa 1960, a club he rescued from a trashcan. He's about a twelve handicap. When it was over, I couldn't tell if he'd enjoyed himself. He paid the caddies and tipped them very nicely. Then he went back to work—if he'd ever left it.

He obviously loves to work. Later, I asked Brenda whether she foresees a little less stress and a little more rest for her husband, or at least concentration on this one grand project, Sage Valley. Well, yes and no, she replied. "I think he's mellowing, just from this setting, from being out here. But trust me: that brain's still working on deals."

His first deal involved a lawn mower.

Chapter 1

SQUARE

The mill provided a job and was good to its employees. They furnished recreation, ball teams, movie theaters. Back then, that was a good-payin' job. Mill people were unique: hard working, loyal, honest.

But you know the line from that old song, 'I owe my soul to the company store'? It was really like that.

—Weldon Wyatt

THE PACOLET MANUFACTURING COMPANY, OF PACOLET,
S.C., CAN FURNISH STEADY EMPLOYMENT FOR OVER 300 DAYS IN
THE YEAR FOR BOYS AND GIRLS OVER 12 YEARS OLD, MEN AND
WOMEN AT AVERAGE WAGES, AS FOLLOWS: EXPERIENCED 12 TO
16-YEAR OLD BOYS AND GIRLS FROM $.50 TO $1.25 [A DAY].
EXPERIENCED BOYS AND GIRLS OVER 16, AND MEN AND WOMEN,
$.75 TO $1.50. OLD MEN, 60 TO 70 YEARS OLD, $.75 TO $1.
WE WANT WHOLE FAMILIES WITH AT LEAST THREE WORKERS FOR
THE MILL IN EACH FAMILY.

—AN EARLY TWENTIETH-CENTURY RECRUITMENT
FLYER FOUND IN NORTH CAROLINA

Pacolet.

If you've been there or lived there, you know not to
pronounce the middle syllable. And you know that this little burg
southeast of Spartanburg is really three connected towns: Pacolet, Central Pacolet, and Pacolet Mills. Locals always joked that
you could drive as fast as you wanted through Central because
the unincorporated village between the other two didn't have a
police force.

But nowadays there's no need to speed. The Pacolet trinity reclines in a verdant river valley—of the Pacolet River, of course—and time drowses by. There's a picture- postcard bridge, a few brick and mortar remnants of an almost forgotten past, and a restoration committee. The town is thick with trees and crisscrossed by two lane streets. Tracks owned by the Norfolk and Southern railway bi-sect the whole thing. It's peaceful and pretty and lightly populated. Nothing happens.

Yet abandoned mills exert a powerful, almost post-Apocalyptic aura, whether they rolled steel in Cleveland or turned cotton into cloth in South Carolina. It's not hard to picture the beehive Pacolet once was when you look at the mural of Pacolet Mill Number Five in what's now City Hall. From Mayor Elaine Harris's window there's a clear view of the concrete pad upon which the gigantic red brick box stood. Today's municipal building was once the heart of the mill—personnel and the bank—and the superintendent sat where Mayor Harris taps the keys on her laptop. The boss of any textile mill was a god-like figure, and no one ever looked the part more than James Ripley "Rip" Westmoreland during his Depression era tenure. Rip's son inherited his father's stern good looks, and showed them to the world when he became the most famous son of Pacolet. As Vietnam Field Commander and then the Army Chief of

——WHEN HE NEEDED SHOES, HIS FATHER MEASURED HIS FOOT WITH A STICK, THEN TOOK THE STICK TO THE COMPANY STORE——

Staff, William Westmoreland was in the news nearly every day from 1964 to 1972, not often in a good way.

The other nationally known Pacolet native was Ernie White, whose high-water mark in thirty years in professional baseball came the day he pitched the St. Louis Cardinals to a 2-0 win over the New York Yankees in the 1941 World Series. Partly due to alphabetized seating in school, and partly because they just liked each other, White's son Joe Dan always seemed to be by Weldon Wyatt's side. If Weldon wasn't at Joe Dan's house, Joe Dan was at his. Their parents worked in the mill.

"*Everybody* worked for the mill, one way or another," recalls Joe Dan White, who is retired from the concrete business and living in Chattanooga. "Even my dad, who pitched for the mill team. It was a very socialistic system that made everybody extremely close. We just took care of each other. I don't think I ever saw a fight."

Weldon's mother's people, the Howells, had come to Pacolet Mills from North Carolina, attracted, perhaps, by an advertisement such as the one that begins this chapter. The Howell family entered a remarkably self-contained universe. The mill provided every government service—police, fire, school, water— plus electricity, entertainment, child care, recreation, and, up to a point, religion. The company store carried all the usual consumer items (at fancy prices), but you didn't need money—all you had to do was sign a coupon. You handed your list to a clerk, who gathered your beans and beef and coal and talcum powder. Mr. Allen Porter loaded the stuff on a horse-drawn wagon and delivered it later that day. Weldon Wyatt remembers that when he needed shoes, his father measured his foot with a stick, took the stick to the store, and came back with his new leather. At one end of the bridge there was a gas station where you could get ice, a burger, and fuel—even the gas station took coupons. And that easy credit combined with low wages was how many mill workers came to owe their soul to the company store.

But whatever their shortcomings—and they were profound—textile mills were the saviors of the post-war South. Perhaps the mill system saved South Carolina's bacon more than any because no state suffered more in the Civil War. About a third of the state's white adult population died during the four years of combat. You could hire substitutes to fight for you: about 15,000 Virginia gentlemen did, but fewer than eight hundred South Carolinians subbed out. Columbia, occupied by troops under the command of General William T. Sherman, burned the night of February 17, 1865. Charleston surrendered that same day. When the smoke cleared, half the state's wealth had been wiped out.

Sharecropping replaced the plantation system, but it was only slavery by another name. The mills were better. They arrived in force in the 1880s, by rivers like the Pacolet, for the power.

Weldon Wyatt's mother Estoy was the sixth of the seven Howell children (an eighth died as an infant). It was Lat, Laura, Lilly Belle, Willie Mae, Doug, Estoy, and Robert. She started work in the Pacolet mill at age fourteen, and, like everyone, got used to the rhythm of the place. A steam whistle blew at five a.m. to wake the town. It shrilled again at 6:50—time to walk to work. The seven o'clock whistle told you to start your machine, and more toots indicated lunch,

lunch over, and quittin' time. Hours were long, pay was low, and the Depression allowed management to pressure employees on both fronts. Doffing was the usual job for newbies and children, that is, removing bobbins when they were full of thread, and replacing them with empties. Virtually every type of mill work was repetitive and, if not exactly dangerous, unhealthy. Years before anyone had heard of OSHA or air conditioning, and with union rules and child-labor laws routinely subverted, mill hands breathed bad air while clattering machines assaulted their ears. Pieces of cotton and thread flew through the air, stuck to bodies and clothes, and lead to the pejorative nickname of lintheads for mill workers.

The Howells owned their own house and rented rooms to help make ends meet. Despite the size of the family, they were a quiet, reserved bunch. But they took in this border in about 1933, Mr. Hayden Wyatt, who…wasn't. His enthusiasm for people and life and the Lord could not be contained. Everybody liked him. Opposites attracted, and Hayden and Estoy were married on December 7, 1934.

Their second child was born in July 1939 in a farmhouse owned by Estoy's sister Laura West and her husband. Mammy West was the midwife. Trains on the uncomfortably close rail line rattled outside, but the baby was quiet, like his mother. They named him Weldon Eugene, after a minister friend of Hayden's.

Our Town was the big new hit when Weldon Wyatt was born, a play and book by Thornton Wilder that expressed the joys and the unutterable ache of life in a small town. But one-industry mill towns ratcheted up the closeness way past Wilder's imagined Grover's Corner, New Hampshire. The title of one of the best and best-known books on the subject tells the tale: *Like a Family: The Making of a Southern Mill World.* It wasn't just that everyone helped and understood each other, and had the same employer, and that locking one's door was almost laughable. These factory towns really were a world and a family, but it was a world with a dictator in its center. Plant superintendents routinely employed spies, who monitored such things as church attendance and drinking.

But Weldon Wyatt and his best pal Joe Dan White thrived. Joe Dan, in particular, recalls an idyllic boyhood in Pacolet. As World War II came and went, he and Weldon hunted crawfish in the creeks and played the sport then in season. School interrupted this Tom Sawyer life—pleasantly, at least for Joe Dan: "Our teachers lived in apartments a hundred yards from the school. The mill built and owned the apartments and the school, and paid the teachers. And they had someone look out for the single teachers like a mother hen.... The teachers were very caring, gave you more pats on the head than swats on the butt. We got an excellent education."

But Weldon didn't like that aspect of his early life. "I couldn't concentrate," he says. "School didn't catch my interest, except history, and there were certain parts of history I didn't like. I was not interested in education."

Hayden Wyatt, Weldon's father, was enduring a similar unease. The gregarious man made them roll in the aisles with his blackface comedy in various mill performances. In time, however, he left the mill to work for the Western Auto store in Pacolet, and, after that, he opened up a used-car lot. But neither thespianship nor selling Studebakers scratched his deepest itch. Perhaps his desire to combine his gift for communication with his deep Christian faith came to a head during one of the late July-through-August intervals farmers called "lay-by time," the period between the cultivation of cotton and corn and their harvest. That was when revivals popped up. Itinerant preachers put up a tent, and, twice a day for a week—at eleven a.m. and seven-thirty p.m.—they revived.

"We called them camp meetings," Wyatt recalls. "They were usually kicked off with dinner on the ground [a picnic]. Whole families attended, including ours. Yes, there was a social aspect to it."

Hayden solved his dilemma in a very direct and modern way: he drove to Gaffney, about nine miles away, and bought time on WAGI, and preached through a microphone into the night air. He had a reasonable, persuasive style, never resorting to fire and brimstone, and his occasional radio ministry continued for about four years. In 1952, a deacon at a Baptist church near Chesnee, South Carolina heard the man from Pacolet and liked what he heard so much that he drove to the radio station to meet him. Would you, the man asked, be interested in preaching at our church?

A prayer had been answered. Yes, Hayden said, he would like to be able to affect a group of people directly, to tend his own flock. And Chesnee was home for him, the town where his parents lived still. So, suddenly, the Wyatts were moving to Chesnee—or, to be more precise, to Mayo, in suburban Chesnee. Just twenty miles north, but a world away.

By this time there were four Wyatt children—Dennis, seventeen; Weldon, thirteen; Joe, seven; and Judy, not yet three. "Dennis was already working and planning on going in the Air

Force. Joe didn't care, and Judy was hardly more than a baby. But I was devastated about the move," Weldon Wyatt says. "Pacolet was all I'd ever known."

But he didn't argue or beg. He went and made the most of it.

Chesnee didn't rate a mention in Walter Edgar's *South Carolina: A History* or any of several other books about the textile industry. Today it's not as pretty and secluded as Pacolet—it's just a Dollar General and a Bi-Lo and a McDonald's on a quiet highway in the foothills near the North Carolina line. But in '52 the town had a mill and a high school on a hill and up the road a ways, Hayden's new employer, Broad River Baptist. Young Weldon adjusted to his new surroundings in two constructive ways: by getting absorbed into sports—particularly basketball—and by making a buck.

—HE'D NEVER FORGET THE BUILDING SO LARGE IT COULD BE MEASURED IN ACRES, AND COTTON FLYING THROUGH THE STUFFY AIR LIKE SNOW FLURRIES—-

The day Hayden took his second son down to the Western Auto where he worked part-time was a milestone in family history. The boy had his eye on a $49 lawn mower. A deal was struck: for a few dollars down and a pledge to pay $2 a week, Weldon walked out with the mower and a business. "I just knocked on doors and said, 'Do you want me to cut your lawn?'" he recalls. "I never was bashful." The debt was retired before the end of summer, far earlier than Western Auto or his father expected. "That was when I knew Weldon would be successful," Hayden told everyone years later.

But success in school eluded him; in fact, he found Chesnee High to be a colossal bore. Except for one subject: basketball. Size—he'd reached his adult height of five foot seven—and disposition made him a point guard, the quarterback position.

School days were divided into six one-hour periods. The basketball coach, Mr. Garner, saw skill and attitude he liked in the boy from Pacolet, so he fixed it so that he'd be in the gym for periods five and six. Liked him so much, in fact, that he gave him a new pair of Chuck Taylor Converse All-Star basketball shoes, footwear he knew his point guard could not afford. "They were white, and they sure looked good," Wyatt recalls with a smile. "Basically, after lunch, all I did was play basketball. I loved it."

And he loved keeping a fashionable appearance, a crucial matter for a high-school kid, but a challenge for a family on a tight budget. "Back then, it was important to have real starched jeans," Wyatt says. "So every day after school I'd wash my jeans, and put steel rods in them while they dried to stretch 'em out and give 'em a good crease. People thought I always had new jeans, but it was the same pair."

Wyatt got a driver's license as soon as he turned fourteen in order to get a job several rungs up from pushing that mower: the Saturday delivery boy for a local general store. "Everything from hog feed to kerosene to groceries," Wyatt recalls. "From seven am to ten pm. They paid me five dollars plus all I could eat." He divvied his sawbuck thusly: a dollar to his mom, for the family budget; fifty cents—a tithe—for the collection plate on Sunday; and the balance to keep himself in creased jeans and eating lunch every day. Girls liked him. Coach Garner liked him. The fact that Joe Dan had also left their old hometown for Spartanburg eased the sting of moving still further, and Pacolet receded into the past. It was then that Hayden dropped another bombshell.

Because he'd never had any formal training in homiletics, evangelism, ethics, theology, or the Bible, and to improve his and his family's prospects, he'd enrolled in the Fruitlands Baptist Bible Institute—"Preaching Is Our Passion"—in Hendersonville, North Carolina, about fifteen miles south of Asheville. It was too long a drive to commute every day; he'd have to stay up there during the week, and come home only on weekends to preach what he'd practiced. His course of study would require three years. With Dennis now in the service, Weldon, at age fourteen, became the man of the house.

Was he ready for his new role? Hayden obviously thought so. Of his four children, his second son was the most like his reserved, self-contained mother. The other three were varying shades of himself—friendly, happy, never met a stranger. An uncle, named Jess, had nicknamed Weldon "Square." The precise meaning has been lost in the family lore, but perhaps Square meant exact, or precise, or "on the square," that is,honest. Judy thinks it could have implied "square peg-round hole," in other words, someone who didn't quite fit in. Whatever it was, the connotations were positive, and the name stuck. And Hayden turned out to be right: Square could handle the responsibility.

"Those three years had a lot to do with how I turned out," Wyatt recalls. "I learned to be as self-sufficient as possible."

But he didn't only take care of himself. Estoy went to work in the Reeves Brothers Textiles mill—as a spinner, on the third shift, eleven pm until seven in the morning. So it fell to Weldon to get breakfast for his mother, his two siblings, and himself, and to take care of Joe and Judy after school so their mother could get some sleep. Occasionally the boy took a meal to his mother at the mill. He'll never forget the building so large it could be measured in acres, and the stuffy air (especially on upper floors in the summer) and bits of cotton flying like snow flurries or confetti. The looms and spools clattered loudly and without pause.

Wyatt helped a lot at home, but he truly ran the show for Coach Moody Garner and the Chesnee Eagles basketball team. An artist would need just three colors to paint his portrait: black and gold, for the uniform, and red, for his face. "He played guard, I played center," recalls Dean Jones. "We had a couple of years together on varsity. We always won. Chesnee was mediocre in football, and less than that in baseball. We were a basketball school.

"Weldon could do it all. None of us was Michael Jordan, but he was a good player—feisty, quick—and he played real hard. It was fun for me if we won, but he played *to* win."

Jones, who stayed on in Chesnee and became the high school's athletic director and baseball coach, remembers it all so well. How the players were scared to death of Coach Garner, who demanded attention by speaking almost in a whisper. Of playing for the Piedmont Conference championship, and winning it. And of the little gyms with rock maple floors and crescent-shaped white wooden backboards, and the games—usually wins— against Cowpens, Boiling Springs, Blacksburg, Inman, and Pacolet (Wyatt, however, does not remember any games against his old school). Based in part on the victories Jones and Wyatt and their teammates helped him compile, Coach Garner made the South Carolina basketball coaches' Hall of Fame. Glory days....

A church that needs a new minister forms a pulpit committee composed of a handful of parishioners willing to hit the road on Sunday morning to attend services elsewhere. They're scouting, basically, and everyone in the visited church knows or soon finds out who the strangers are.

Howlandville Baptist in Graniteville, South Carolina needed a spiritual leader, and they'd heard good things about a new graduate of Fruitlands Baptist Bible who preached at a little church just over the North Carolina line. So their pulpit committee journeyed 120 miles northeast to attend services at Broad River Baptist one Sunday in February 1955. They were impressed by the content and delivery of the sermon and that the minister didn't refer to his notes even once (actually, he had no notes; Hayden Wyatt never committed his thoughts to paper). Handshakes all around when it was over, and how are you, Mrs. Wyatt, and hello, Weldon, Joe, and you must be Judy. They extended an invitation for Hayden to come down to Graniteville the next Sunday to preach at their church and to have a look around.

The five Wyatts loaded into their blue '49 Chevrolet Bel-Air early in the morning six days later. Graniteville—it couldn't have been a surprise—turned out to be another mill town.

CHAPTER 2

THE CORPS

THE TWO BIGGEST IMPACTS ON MY LIFE

WERE MY FAITH

AND THE UNITED STATES MARINE CORPS.

—WELDON WYATT

A little more than a month after the visit to Howlandville Baptist, the Wyatts moved into the square plain parsonage next door to the square plain church. Weldon had left behind his beloved coach, his teammates, and a girlfriend. He went reluctantly but without complaint. The classic image of the rebellious preacher's son never fit him.

In several ways, the almost-sixteen-year old was poorly prepared to be dropped into a new school. Basketball season was over, so he wouldn't be winning admirers while helping the Graniteville Rocks win games. He was not an exceptionally outgoing kid, not the type to introduce himself to potential new friends. And the albatross of an academic record he bore in from Chesnee would not have made his new teachers eager with the prospect of a bright new student. His grades were like the set-up to an old joke. He'd made D-minus in English 1, English 2, World History and Algebra; F in Biology; and Cs in General Science and World Geography. His lone good grade had been an A in Phys Ed. "Son," a football coach says in the joke, while looking at a similar record from one of his players, "you're obviously spending too much time on one subject."

And the culture at Leavelle McCampbell (Graniteville) High was inevitably a little different from the one he'd just left. The 1955 yearbook, *The Strata*, detailed the changes everyone at school had faced, and the new kid tried to absorb in three months:

> ...the new cafeteria and gymnatorium were completed... activity period changed to the middle of the day...Graniteville High had an exchange teacher from England and a full-time music teacher...the boys went all-out for pink and black...the girls wore princess-style dresses or acquired that boyish look with v-neck sweaters...the Rocks beat Aiken in the Cotton Festival Game...everybody went mambo crazy...it snowed for the first time since 1944....

The boys rolled up their jeans about four inches—they didn't do that at Chesnee—and wore their hair in ornate Elvis-influenced 'dos. Perhaps due to sensory overload, today Wyatt has no memory of either of the two Most Likely to Succeed: Ruthy Rae Smith and Sonny McDaniel—or the amazing Willie Belle Carter, whose classmates elected the Most Talented, Best Dressed, Most Athletic, Object of Desire, and Homecoming Queen. He can recall Verley Swygert, the quarterback for the Rocks, who was something of a celebrity, and Bob Platt and Danny Marchant. But that's it.

"She was tough, a fine lady," he says of the only Graniteville High teacher he can recall, Ms. Eulalie G. Busbee. Ms. Busbee taught Algebra to the boy from Chesnee. Unsuccessfully. She gave him an F.

In June, on the last day of school, young Weldon Wyatt turned right out of the driveway at the rectory and walked a downhill mile on tree-canopied Howlandville Road. Just past the railroad tracks and this side of a canal, he turned right again. The high school, a solid block of red brick with accents of local granite and white wood trim, squatted directly across the street from the massive and venerable Graniteville mill. He went inside, came out some hours later, and never returned.

"Quitting school back then was nothing unusual," Wyatt says. "My parents didn't want me to, but they knew I didn't have no interest in it."

Hindsight confirms that the boy—he turned sixteen that July—was not as unprepared for life as the run of the mill dropout. The first positive was that he didn't just walk across the street to the employment office at Graniteville mill; he knew he didn't want that life. Moreover, he'd proved his mettle during his father's three years in seminary. He'd also absorbed Hayden's willingness to think big and to be flexible—exemplified by his radio ministry, and his dropping everything at age forty-one to attend Fruitlands Baptist Bible Institute. The underlying strengths in Hayden were his belief in hard work and God, and those were his son's trump cards, too.

So Weldon did what he'd done before, only harder. He got a job with Marvin and Ed Walton, brothers who owned Piggly Wiggly grocery stores in the contiguous small towns of Graniteville, Warrenville, and Vaucluse. He stocked shelves, sorted produce, and drove the delivery truck. Every day he passed or drove through land that would become Sage Valley half a century later. After a year of getting $35 a week from the Waltons, he took a similar job with a local A & P for $55 a week. Then—a red-letter day—he made his first deal, one that provided a template for a lot of what he did in the future. He bought low, added value, knew his market, and sold high.

"A farmer had an old '47 Chevy for sale, and he wanted a hundred and twenty-five dollars for it," Wyatt recalls. "I'd saved up seventy-five dollars, so I offered him that. He said no, so I walked away. He said wait, I'll finance the difference. I said, no, seventy-five, and he took it.

"The car was very dirty, but at least it had seat covers. I took off those covers and beat the seats with a broom handle every day for a week. It looked like I'd turned on a fogger in there. I cleaned that car for two or three weeks and then I put a for sale sign on it. When I came home from work one day, someone had paid full price for it—four hundred and seventy-five dollars. Right then I was working forty-two and a half hours a week for fifty-five dollars. I said 'Man, do I like that!'"

As Wyatt's teens became his twenties, and the odometer on the 1950s prepared to turn over, national and world events abruptly became a concern. Every American kid had a vague idea that a very big country, the Union of Soviet Socialist Republics, was dedicated to our destruction and might any day lob a nuclear bomb onto New York or Los Angeles or Spartanburg. People built fallout shelters and wrestled with what to do with neighbors stuck on the surface when the worst occurred; eventually, handguns were thought to be as essential in the family bunker as chemical toilets and canned food. A market for lead and metal foil undergarments emerged. Every schoolboy and girl endured faintly comic, faintly tragic civil-defense drills, in which students were required to crawl under their desks at the sound of an alarm, and cover their heads with their arms. Anyone who dared to think about this practice recognized its futility against nuclear fire or radiation.

A person at age twenty in 1959—as Wyatt was—had no direct recollection of the Depression, and only the haziest memories of World War II. But this thing about Godless Communists, and their desire to take over the world—that was real. Civil-defense drills and the Korean War proved it. And then a new metaphor, first used by President Eisenhower in 1954, became the easy-to-grasp linchpin of American foreign policy. Allowing even one little country in Southeast Asia to fall to the Communists, Ike said, might result in a sequential loss of all the Western allies in the Pacific, "like a row of dominoes." The one little country he was referring to was Vietnam. Weldon Wyatt was not in college in 1961, not holding down a vital defense job, and not married. He was, in short, a perfect candidate for the United States military draft.

෨

The success with the '47 Chevy flip encouraged Wyatt to try his second go-it-alone business, a service station. He bought, sold and repaired cars on a lot in Aiken, the family having moved there in 1957.

Never had the Wyatts lived in such a town. Although just a few miles away from Graniteville, Aiken's old money allowed a horsey set—the town once billed itself as "The Winter Polo Capital of America"—gorgeous hotels and mansions, and a superb golf club, Palmetto. To the sons and daughters of elevated Aiken, people who lived in Graniteville, Warrenville, and other towns down around Horse Valley Creek were quite literally beneath them. "Valley rats" was the nickname. An Aiken kid might take a summer job picking peaches in Edgefield or toiling in that very big building in Graniteville—becoming, temporarily, a mill rat—but Aiken was the place to be in this part of South Carolina.

With a bit of time and money for the first time in his life, Wyatt considered golf. He watched Nelson, Snead, Hogan, and other stars of the professional golf tour at the precursor for the Masters, the Palmetto Pro-Am, whose Calcutta often yielded more money for the winner than the Masters. An intoxicating bouquet filled the air: the scent of good perfume, polite but fierce competition, and wealth. Fred Astaire had played Palmetto, as did the King of England, and Harry Vardon. Augusta National founders Jones and Roberts had taken on the tight old course frequently—particularly when their own track was under construction. According to Stan Byrdy's *Augusta and Aiken in Golf's Golden Age,* at least six Palmetto members were charter members at the National. With all this to inspire him, Wyatt bought a set of K-Mart golf clubs, which he'd eventually replace with Hogans, around the same time he joined Palmetto. Basketball players always seem to find their way to golf.

But geopolitics intruded on his consciousness. The relentless competition between the Communist world and the United States—always with overtones of restrained violence— was unavoidable to anyone who turned on a radio or TV or opened a newspaper. Sometimes the violence was real, as in the Bay of Pigs fiasco in April 1961, or in Vietnam. It was war and rumors of war, to use the Biblical phrase, and a polarized country far removed from the placid national mood of the '50s. "There are two groups of frustrated citizens," President Kennedy said. "It is a curious fact that each resembles the other. Each believes that we have only two choices: appeasement or war, suicide or surrender, humiliation or holocaust, to be either Red or dead."

Weldon Wyatt also had two choices: get drafted or enlist. The uncertainty of his life caused him to "kinda float for a year. I took a job with Dixie Tire Company. I couldn't commit.... Then a friend said to me, 'let's join the Reserves and avoid the draft.'"

Why the Marines? "Because they were recruiting heavily," Wyatt replies. "They wanted us, and the Army reserves was full." Why the Reserves? The benefits were obvious: in exchange for a long, drawn-out commitment, Reserve units were usually called into combat situations only when there weren't enough drafted troops. "The idea was to avoid going to Vietnam," Wyatt says, "not go to Vietnam."

—"WHEN THOSE DRILL INSTRUCTORS STARTED HOLLERIN', I REMEMBER HOW SCARED I WAS"—

The first week in January 1962, the twenty-one year-old car and tire salesman reported to the Marine Corps Recruit Depot at Parris Island, at the southern tip of the state, for the most intense military training anywhere. Retracing his steps from Aiken to the coast may provide some insight into what he saw and felt, and, given the importance to him of those three-plus months, the experience deserves a bit of scrutiny.

Wyatt and the other potential Marines met a bus in Augusta at about eight p.m. and arrived without stops about two hours later. The landscape flattened twenty miles out as the soil turned to sand, and the bus headlights illuminated the grotesque, moody beauty of oak trees draped with Spanish moss. Mobile-home parks dotted the land on the unprepossessing approach to the base. That first night, Wyatt would have sensed, rather than seen, the forbidding five thousand acre salt marsh surrounding Parris Island.

The night arrival was a purposeful, immediate effort to disorient with sleep deprivation. The bus pulled up to the Recruit Receiving Station. With its nine wide concrete steps leading up to a brick edifice, it looked like a small-town post office. "Back then, everybody smoked, which wasn't allowed, so there was a scramble to get rid of the cigarettes," Wyatt recalls. "Then those drill instructors started hollerin' at you. I remember how frightened I was."

Inside the Receiving Station, the recruits—"boots"—followed the well-worn path of haircut, uniform issuance, and being shouted at by someone very good at shouting. This was not substantially different from the fierce welcomes from other branches of the military, but then the quantity and insistence of the Marine Corps Drill Instructor's barking accelerated past imagining. And the physical demands—running long distances with a fifty-five pound pack; swimming fully clothed; climbing ropes; running obstacle courses; rappelling; jousting with pugil sticks; firing a rifle accurately; keeping oneself and one's gear "squared away"; standing at attention while a mosquito bites your face and not slapping it—all this done on reduced sleep—surpassed the demands of the Army, Navy, Coast Guard or Air Force. Semper Fi, the drill instructors said, and "Let no man's ghost say 'I wasn't trained well enough.'"

Everything was done in groups, units, teams. Midway through their three-plus months, boots erase personal pronouns from their vocabularies. "This recruit won't give up," they say. "This recruit thinks this is the toughest thing he's ever done."

Because six recruits had literally been trained to death in April 1956—a drill sergeant had marched his underperforming unit, Platoon 71, into Ribbon Creek in the middle of the night—Wyatt believes that his class had it relatively easy. But none of it was really easy. He "enjoyed"—looking back—the intricacy and discipline of drill, and the wonderful look of precision marching. He did extremely well on the rifle range and qualified as an Expert. "Of course, I don't think you really *like* any of it," he says. "But the thing that really got to you was getting out of bed in the dark and having to run two miles around the parade ground before breakfast." He persevered and got through it all. He'd weighed 130 pounds on the bus going into Parris Island and was fairly fit but undefined. After thirteen weeks of care and feeding by the United States Marine Corps, he was 145 pounds, muscular, and in the best physical shape of his life.

Probably the greatest achievement of Marine Corps training is its team-building, its esprit de corps. But that comes with a paradox: great teams are composed of individuals focusing very intently on *themselves* and their own high performance. That leaders require nothing so much as followers is another lesson of the military experience. Group dynamics remains a subtle thing, in other words. When it works, it's a balancing act, understood by successful people, and by ex-Marines.

His proud parents and sister Judy came down for the graduation ceremony on an abnormally hot day in April—which was tough, because the new Marines were still in their blue-wool dress uniforms. Wyatt stood ramrod straight and unflinching as sweat rolled down his back and sand fleas flew into his nose and eyes.

And then it was over. From Parris Island, he shipped to Camp Lejeune in North Carolina for Infantry Training—to learn how to fight. The thirteen weeks of boot camp and the warrior school at Camp Lejeune counted toward the required six months of active duty. For the next eight years, Wyatt would have to report to a base one weekend a month, plus participate in an annual two-week bivouac. His base—blessedly close to Aiken—would be Fort Gordon, near Augusta, in a vehicle-maintenance unit. For most of the '60s, while the most unpopular war in American history built to a boil, he was a soldier ready to be deployed on short notice.

The Marines had grafted new steel in his spine.

"The Marine Corps had a great impact on me," Wyatt says. "That experience matured me and gave me self-discipline I didn't have before. My values changed. Suddenly, I had a lot of confidence. There were not many things I was afraid to do."

CHAPTER 3

BRENDA

GOD GIVES EVERY BIRD HIS WORM, BUT HE

DOES NOT THROW IT INTO THE NEST.

—SWEDISH PROVERB

*H*e was in real estate and a leisure suit. White shoes, belt and shirt, and the collar on the shirt extended like wings out past his clavicle. He sat in the Man O' War Lounge in the Surrey Center on Berkmans Road in Augusta. The MOW was

new, clean, and the best place around to see and be seen in
1976. It had a U-shaped bar in the center of the room, a dance
floor (and dance contests), live bands from time to time, and the
whole panoply of disco-era lights and sounds. Abba was big, and
the Ohio Players, and K.C. and the Sunshine Band. You'd hear
Wild Cherry's "Play That Funky Music" five times a night, if you
stayed long enough. Wyatt never stayed long enough. He didn't
dance, didn't like the out-of-control feeling of too much alcohol,
wasn't really a man about town.

But he was out on the town when she came in, a dark-
haired beauty from Aiken. They knew each other but had never
really talked. "Hi, Weldon. Hi, y'all," Brenda Grice said to Wyatt
and his friends as she walked toward the dance floor. In those
days, Ms. Grice would rather dance than eat.

Wyatt called her the next day to test that proposition:
would she eat lunch with him? No, she said, I can't—but with
enough genuine regret in her voice
that her suitor tried again the
next day. They had lunch.
Then they had dinner at
the Good Dale Inn in
Beech Island, South
Carolina, James
Brown's hometown,
where the food was
simple, just as he
liked.

"My father
was just thrilled when he
heard I was going out with
Weldon," recalls Brenda.

"He didn't know him that well, but you can know someone's character."

That was June. In July, after dining on moo goo gai pan and fortune cookies, Wyatt glided his date home in his white, late-model Cadillac. He stopped for a red light. On impulse, Brenda slid up close and planted a big old kiss on the surprised driver, then slid back when the light turned green.

"What do you think about a steady dose of each other?" Wyatt said in the driveway. His leisure suit that night was beige.

Long pause. "Leading to m-m-marriage?" Brenda asked.

"That's right." Longer pause.

Brenda agreed to think it over. She said good night and entered the house. Like a sleepwalker, she got a box of Oreos and a glass of milk from the kitchen and sat in the dark on a rocker in the living room. "Darling, what's wrong?" her mother asked.

Brenda was the daughter of Hastings Grice, the pre-eminent butcher in Aiken, the inventor of the extra-meaty Yankee spare rib. She was divorced, with a daughter, Ashley, five. Wyatt, too, was divorced, with a daughter, Ramona, who lived with her mother. Brenda was outgoing. Weldon always thought before he spoke. He liked the Bee Gees. She liked the Bee Gees. They both belonged to the Baptist Church. Their attraction was mutual. They were perfect for each other, but the sincerity and decisiveness that were two of Wyatt's best traits were making the relationship progress with speed that frightened Brenda. He asked her to marry while they were sitting on the couch in his parents' house. That was August.

ରେ

Weldon Wyatt's role model was his father.

Almost all their lives, the children of Hayden Wyatt sat in a pew on Sunday and listened to their father discuss life, faith, and the Lord. "Dad was the ultimate salesman," Judy says. "Selling the unseen and the unknown...He never believed in condemnation. He didn't think you can hurt people or make them angry and bring them to Christ. And he believed every word he said. He didn't wait until Saturday night or until he was standing in the pulpit to lead a moral life."

Since ministers' jobs at small churches paid peanuts, Hayden always had to do something else to supplement the family income. He invariably chose sales. "P.T. Barnum wasn't the greatest salesman in the world," Judy says. "My dad was." He also launched a couple of start-ups, such as Snazzy's, an Age of Aquarius purveyor of designer jeans and polyester casual clothes. The principles he applied to sell a car or a suit of clothes echoed what he said on Sundays and how he said it: Be honest. Believe in what you're selling. People do business with people they like. Weldon Wyatt still quotes his father on the issues of punctuality ("if you say you're going to be in the town square at noon, be there waiting at eleven fifty-five"); humility ("no matter how big you get, you have to put your pants on one leg at a time"); and random chance ("success comes from who you know, and timing"). It wasn't all original or snappy but all of it stuck in his son's mind.

As soon as Weldon Wyatt completed his active duty in the Marines in June 1962, he and his father went into business together: Wyatt's New and Used Cars. "At first we used the parking lot next door to a convenience store on Richland Avenue [in Aiken], near Union Street," Wyatt recalls. "Then we bought a piece of property at Richland and Horry, and re-located there. We sold a lot of late-model stuff that we bought from dealers and at auctions. But the big thing for us was Volkswagen."

There was money to be made in the days before VW had dealers. The little German car had been introduced to the United States in 1949, and its popularity grew slowly but steadily. The manufacturer in Wolfsburg upgraded a little each year for the American market—a bigger rear window, better turn signals, smoother transmissions, more chrome. The Wyatts took the Beetles off the ship in Jacksonville twenty at a time.

It didn't take long before the Wyatts were seeking a bigger sale and markup than an economy car offered. In 1966 Hayden and Weldon cast their eyes on the burgeoning mobile home business. They disbanded Wyatt's New and used Cars to start a company called—what else—Wyatt's Mobile Homes. They parked the aluminum domiciles on their Richland Avenue lot until moving to more spacious quarters on Highway 1. Eventually, they had four lots around Aiken.

Now, instead of pointing out the advantages and benefits of a Synchromesh transmission, Wyatt informed a new set of potential buyers that this particular model of mobile home, the Valhalla, had three bedrooms, one-and-a-half baths, a drywall ceiling, and stove and refrigerator included. Town and Country Mobile Homes of Wichita Falls, Texas was their primary supplier (a minor supplier, North Carolina-based Taylor Manufacturing, would become important to Wyatt a few years later). Buying and selling cars was similar to selling manufactured housing, but the stakes were far higher. For example: full retail on a mid-'60s VW, after transportation from the port of Jacksonville and a thorough wash in Aiken, was $1695. "If someone came in with cash, our profit was only twenty dollars," Wyatt recalls. "Where you made your money was on the trade-ins, and financing." But large, illiquid houses cost many times as much as a Volkswagen and seldom involved a trade-in. "You'd buy for twenty (thousand dollars) and try to sell for thirty," says Wyatt. "We had a lot of debt."

Both Wyatts met the customers and made the deals, but Hayden had less time to devote than his son, busy as he was with his duties as the pastor at Couchton Baptist in Aiken.

The senior Wyatt manned the till admirably during his son's one-weekend-a-month, two-weeks-a-summer commitment to the Marines, but at heart, the business was a one-man show. Its slow pace and long hours gave Weldon Wyatt plenty of time to take stock.

His daily preoccupation was the steadily bigger, hotter war in Vietnam. American investments in dollars and manpower were making quantum leaps every year. Troop levels topped 200,00 in 1965, 375,000 in 1966, and, by April 1967, 480,000 United States soldiers had their feet on the ground in Vietnam, more than our presence at the height of the Korean War. The pride of Pacolet came home to meet with President Johnson to request more: General Westmoreland wanted to have 680,000 troops by June 1968. These were not mere sterile numbers for a man watching the first televised war in history, a man who had trained with people who were fighting and dying in Da Nang, Hue City, and Khe Sanh. Over 13,000 Marines died in Vietnam.

Wyatt kept himself prepared for the call. Several times, his number was just about up, but he finished his military commitment in 1968 without having to go to 'Nam.

With that bridge crossed, he addressed other concerns. "I was just making a living," he recalls. "I became dissatisfied....I don't know why, but land had always fascinated me. The Lord gives us all talents, but it takes a while to find out what they are. You might need a while to discover what you can do best. Some people never find out. They think they can fly a 747, but they can't."

In March 1971, Wyatt sold the mobile-home company. Hayden went on to Snazzy's; Weldon got a real estate license and went into business with an Aiken man, Mackie Walker, who built and sold houses. The progression seemed logical—selling homes on wheels, then homes on foundations. Wyatt, now thirty-two, began to learn the basics of residential construction and the frustrating facts of life for a real-estate agent. Showing Mr. and Mrs. Smith homes all day, he discovered, was not his cup of tea.

"To sell a house, you had to please four people—the couple who were buying it and both their mothers-in-law," Wyatt says. "The commission was six percent. But the commission for commercial real estate was ten percent, and you only had to please one person, the buyer. So I preferred commercial."

And then—drum roll—in 1972, the mere agent became a developer. A doctor Wyatt knew owned thirty acres in Aiken, and he wanted to sell it for $40,000. Another acquaintance needed ground on which to plant a Pontiac dealership. Wyatt got back to the doctor, telling him that he might want to buy the property himself. Would he accept one thousand dollars for a ninety-day option? He would. Then Wyatt took the potential car dealer to see the land, the elevation of which—at least twenty feet below the street—had caused it to be available at a decent price. High ground is almost always considered more valuable, but Wyatt explained that the low-lying acres could actually be a great benefit to a man selling cars—passersby could easily see the entire inventory. I'd need ten acres, the man said. How much? Forty thousand, Wyatt replied, and the deal was made.

"When the doctor heard what I'd done, he tried to go back on our agreement," Wyatt recalls. "But he checked with his lawyer who told him no, you can't do that.

"I sold the entire thirty acres for $120,000 (a profit of

$80,000). It taught me that you have to believe in what you're doing. And it gave me seed money."

The plant that grew from the seed two years later showcased all Wyatt's skills and self-belief. In some ways, it was his greatest deal.

The transaction—really, set of transactions—began years before, when Wyatt and son were in the mobile-home business. Mr. Taylor, the owner of pre-fab housing builder Taylor Manufacturing, had acquired twenty-eight acres in Aiken at the corner of Pine Log and Whiskey Roads. He let it slip to that nice young fella Weldon Wyatt that he wouldn't mind selling it for the right price, the right price being $10,000 an acre. This was 1966 or 1967, well before Wyatt's coup with the doctor and the Pontiac dealer. He declined Mr. Taylor's offer but filed the information away.

Fast-forward to 1974: South Carolina National Bank had targeted a branch office for Aiken. The bank's representative quite reasonably got in touch with Wyatt, whose name had risen to the top in local real-estate sales. Wyatt called Mr. Taylor.

"Have you still got that land?" he asked.

"Yeah, I've got it."

"Do you still want $10,000 an acre?"

"No," Taylor said. "Twenty thousand."

Wyatt told Taylor what he had in mind, finding just one little acre for a bank. Well, good luck, the man from North Carolina replied, but I'm not selling *one* acre. It's the whole thing or nothing. I'll get back to you, the developer said.

Wyatt reported the good news to South Carolina National: he'd found them the perfect piece of land, on Aiken's fast-growing west side, for $150,000. After the bank had a look and agreed to the price, Wyatt executed a contract to buy Taylor's entire twenty-eight acre, $560,000 parcel. He kept selling—or, said another way, he let the buyers come to him, by encouraging SCN to announce the deal immediately.

—WYATT SAID YES,

HE WOULD BUILD THE

GROCERY STORE—EVEN

THOUGH HE'D NEVER

BUILT ANYTHING IN

HIS LIFE—

The bait worked. Before the sale to South Carolina National closed, while surveyors with transits were driving stakes to mark the boundaries of the new branch office, a representative from Atlanta-based Colonial Foods came calling. I understand you own land out on Pine Log Road, the man said. Would you be interested in building us a Big Star grocery store and leasing it back to us?

With only a moment's hesitation, Wyatt answered yes, he would be very interested in such a deal. But what a gamble! Except for his remote involvement in Walker Realty's construction of three-bed, two-bath houses on a third of an acre, Wyatt hadn't built anything before. But at this crucial moment, he did what he'd always do when he lacked a needed bit of expertise: he hired it. Gilliam Construction of Aiken would oversee the intricate dance of permits and bulldozers, of subcontractors and building codes, and Wyatt would oversee Gilliam's man, Allan Woods. In some ways, it was that '47 Chevy all over again: Wyatt bought at a good price, added value, knew his market, and sold high.

Eventually other tenants—including Revco—filled up the strip shopping center Wyatt built. Actually, it looked like two strips there behind South Carolina National. Seven or eight acres separated one from the other. Perhaps something else could go in there someday.

ൟ

A lot happened in the Bicentennial year. The post-Vietnam, post-Watergate social upheaval left the stage for a minute in favor of the hubbub of the 200th anniversary of the United States. Ribbon cuttings and balloons marked the opening of the new Big Star grocery store at Pine Log and Whiskey Roads. In the presidential election, conservative Aiken was one of only three South Carolina counties not carried by Jimmy Carter. And a new business hung out a shingle: Wyatt Development.

"I thought that I needed to get out on my own," Wyatt recalls. "Mackie Walker was satisfied with what we were doing, but I had a bigger picture.

"So I opened up a little office, just me and my secretary, Ann McGee—she left Mackie to come with me. She became like a sister to me."

Ms. McGee, an Aiken native, had been with Walker Realty two years. She recalls that Mr. Walker and Mr. Wyatt were both in the room for her job interview. "Weldon's a great guy. I have the utmost respect for him," she says. "I thought a lot of Mackie, too. But he was so tight. He really squeezed a dime. He had gotten into government-subsidized housing, while Weldon wanted to focus on commercial business. Yes, it was the unknown, but I saw a better opportunity with Weldon."

But she didn't see much luxury. The first Wyatt Development office was a tiny two-room office building—office shack?—on Pine Log Road. Ms. McGee was not claustrophobic, fortunately, and a wonderful friendship and business relationship began. Now, more than thirty years later, Ann McGee still works part-time for her old boss.

And before 1976 was over, another long-term relationship was formalized at City Hall: Weldon Wyatt married Brenda Grice.

The best break Weldon ever had, according to his sister. "She's been behind him through thick and thin, always backing him one hundred and ten percent," says Judy. "I guarantee a negative word has never passed her lips. Brenda is the *woman*."

CHAPTER 4

I'LL FIND A BEAR, YOU SKIN IT

WELDON REFINED DADDY'S SALES ART.

HE'S A TRUE ENTREPRENEUR—

YOU CAN ALMOST HEAR THE WHEELS

TURNING IN HIS HEAD.

HE'S THE SMARTEST UNEDUCATED MAN

I'VE EVER KNOWN.

—JUDY WYATT PARKER

The gradual then sudden then spectacular success of Weldon Wyatt can be described in a variety of ways. Since he's a very tough but moral man, his rise had a sort of Old Testament ring; perhaps his life amounts to a parable. As one who built his fortune during the go-go years of the two Reagan Administrations, Wyatt could be portrayed as a paragon of '80s capitalism. And we might view his success as an interesting sidelight in the explosive, culture-changing ascent of Wal-Mart.

Another frame of reference suggests itself: athletics. Business is, of course, rife with corny sports metaphors—we're going to blitz the competition!—and retired running backs who retain their powers of speech can make a good living telling attendees at sales meetings that success in the wholesale plumbing-parts business requires the same steps taken by the Steelers when they won the Super Bowl. But Wyatt really did operate like the point guard he once was. He was the facilitator, the determined, selfless, and aggressive leader who put his team in a position to succeed, never caring a whit about glory for himself. The squad he assembled—the builder, the banker, the operations man—defied the odds by getting into the biggest game in the grandest arena. His team from Nowhere, South Carolina gained momentum, overcame adversity, and won the financial equivalent of the championship. Even when Wyatt Development failed on a bleak February day in 1990, it only set the stage for a dramatic last-minute comeback that seemed cinematic, like *Hoosiers* or something from Disney about a hockey or a baseball team.

But the sports comparison ultimately is not worthy. A lot of people had their flesh and blood in this thing. It was more than a game. And it was no movie.

ᏍᎳ

Outside a two-room wood building so modest it made a refrigerator box look grand, the summer sun blazed down on a new white '78 Cadillac. Weldon Wyatt was in his office on Pine Log Road in Aiken.

"We were robbin' Peter to pay Paul in those days, and sometimes it was hard to make the payment on that car," recalls Ann McGee, Wyatt's bookkeeper and secretary. "I'd say, 'Weldon, why do you have to have another new Cadillac?' and he'd say, 'You have to look prosperous to be prosperous.' He'd also say, 'Our day is gonna come, I know it.'"

In an important way, Wyatt's time had already arrived because his family life provided such deep satisfaction. He adored his daughter, Ashley, now age seven. Couldn't have been more proud of his just-born son Tom. Because of age and gender difference, and their gentle temperaments, the two children would never be rivals. Ashley acting as a loving assistant mom deepened the peace at home. Of all of them, Mrs. Wyatt had the biggest job and the most adjustments to make.

"Weldon told me early on, I have two rules,'" Brenda recalls. "Don't say anything about me playin' golf, and don't make me do anything I don't want to do."

The main thing he didn't want to do was go out to dinner, or play bridge at the neighbors house, or do much of anything at night but rest, read, play with the kids, and watch TV. Vacations? No—the Wyatts didn't take one for the first six or seven years of their marriage. "Weldon said, 'I want us to be just as happy sitting on the couch eating a hot dog as going someplace fancy,'" says Brenda, a twinkle in her eye. "That was fine—but I didn't know it would be every night."

So she cooked and quickly discovered the key to her husband's taste: cole slaw. "He eats cole slaw the way other people drink iced tea." Add pinto beans, cornbread from a black cast-iron skillet, some fried green tomatoes, possibly some chicken, and that was a delicious dinner. Mr. Wyatt, however, required greater variety at breakfast, as he enjoyed a rotating selection of biscuits and milk gravy; grits, eggs and bacon; cereal; pancakes; and rice with butter and sugar.

Despite having two young children to care for and no help, Brenda cleaned the house to spotlessness every day.

But except for a debate about the proper preparation of

hoecakes—she fried, his mama had baked—there was very little conflict. Brenda owned the wisdom to recognize contentment and love when they came her way. "I'd always wanted to be a mother and a wife," she says. "And you could never have better kids than Tom and Ashley."

ASHLEY AND WELDON

The dynamics of the other Wyatt family—Hayden and Estoy and their sons and one daughter—evolved in an interesting way. Big, gregarious Dennis, the oldest, had returned to town after a long career in the Air Force. Joe, the hilarious third child, had also come back home—this time for good—from another failed campaign playing professional golf in Florida. He just couldn't beat Calvin Peete. Judy, the youngest sibling, had never left; she married C. E. Parker and settled in Aiken. All of them lived within five miles of each other. And all of them from Hayden on down looked to the quiet one, the ex-Marine, as the leader of the clan. Weldon obviously had a plan and a big future, so it was no surprise when his little brother decided to tag along. Just-divorced Joe joined the development company as the second employee after Ann McGee. His job, Wyatt recalls, was "just to do whatever I asked him to do."

—ALL OF THEM, FROM HAYDEN ON DOWN, LOOKED TO THE EX-MARINE AS THE LEADER OF THE CLAN—

That Joe was a caution. "If Joe was there, there was laughter," recalls Judy. "He was everybody's favorite." Occasionally he'd aggravate his brother with some thing he did or didn't do for Wyatt Development, which would cause Weldon, red-faced and wiggling his finger, to rise from his chair. At which point Joe always joked his way out, defusing the situation so completely that Weldon's anger dissolved into helpless laughter. "The more you laughed, the more he kept on," says Ann McGee.

Although these two brothers could wear each other's clothes, the similarities stopped there. "They were complete opposites," Ann recalls. "Joe was a nice guy and he *loved* to have fun. Weldon was straitlaced. I suppose they complemented each other. Joe wined and dined, and Weldon made the deals."

For Wyatt, a key part of deal-making was reconnaissance. A bit of golf and card playing at Palmetto amounted to networking with the local movers and shakers, and his thirst for reading showed him the world outside Aiken. He knew, or tried to know, who was buying, who was selling and where the best opportunities lay. One weekend in 1980 his eye fell on a feature story in a trade magazine about a regional retailer in Bentonville,

Arkansas. Wal-Mart's niche, the article explained, was big stores, low prices, and small towns, all of them located in increasingly distant concentric rings around the headquarters in little Bentonville. The company was growing like mad: its net income had increased thirty-nine percent the previous year. The chain had 229 stores in ten states and was predicting 1980 sales of a billion dollars.

"The thing that caught my attention was their focus on small towns," recalls Wyatt. "They liked to locate in towns of about five thousand people with a trading area of twenty thousand. I said to myself, these people think the same way I do. Sears and K-Mart, on the other hand, said they needed a trade area of fifty thousand. But when they'd get to that bigger city, they'd find themselves with three or four competitors."

On Monday morning, Wyatt called directory assistance. Dialed the number. "Wal-Mart," said the operator, Arkansas music in her voice. She transferred the call. The head of the real estate and construction division answered his own phone. "Tom Seay," he said.

The conversation between the South Carolinian and the Akansawyer quickly grew very interesting. Wyatt told Seay (pronounced "see") about the shopping center he'd put in the ground, its tenants, and the seven- or eight-acre vacancy in the middle of the property that might be perfect for a big retailer and its parking lot. Seay, impressed, replied positively. We need to talk about this, he said. When can you come to Bentonville?

"That was Monday morning," Wyatt recalls. "I went home to pack my suitcase. Joe and I drove the fourteen hours to Arkansas, and we were in Seay's office at ten a.m. on Wednesday."

Seay remembers it this way: "this guy calls me on a Monday morning to suggest we put a Wal-Mart in Aiken, South Carolina. And I said, you know, we really do want a store in that town. How soon can you get here? Little did I know he was going to *drive*."

Thus, the often-repeated tale that Wyatt had so much pluck and luck that he went to Wal-Mart unannounced and waited all day until he met Sam Walton himself and left with a contract is a mere myth. He had not only an appointment, he had the underpinnings of a deal. Details and approvals had to be worked out, of course, but the financials came down to this: Wal-Mart required a sixty-three thousand square-foot building that Wyatt Development would build and lease back to them for twenty years. Rent would be three dollars and sixty-five cents per foot per year, or $229,050 annually. Wyatt's challenge would be to erect, electrify, and plumb the big box on time and under budget while meeting all the codes and specs from the government and Wal-Mart.

And he did. The blue steel building cost an amazingly low thirteen dollars and seventy-five cents per square foot to build, or $866,250. Let's see, twenty times $229,950 equals (eventually) about $4.6 million, so after three or four years of applying Wal-Mart's rent to the construction loan, Wyatt Development would be in a very nice cash-flow position, and—who knew?—ready to do it again.

Which was exactly how it happened. Wyatt and Wal-Mart really got rolling, and really got to know each other with their second project in Barnwell, South Carolina, in 1984.

Although Wyatt worked with Seay and only indirectly with company founder Sam Walton, it's useful, if not actually intriguing, to compare and contrast the leaders of the two companies; Walton got straight A's in high school. Wyatt didn't. Walton was an eagle scout; Wyatt wasn't a joiner. Sam piloted his own plane; on the ground, he favored beat-up pick-up trucks. Weldon didn't fly; he arrived in a late-model white Cadillac—or a luxury bus. Walton's brother Bud, a Senior Vice President and Director of Wal-Mart, was quiet as a mouse. Joe Wyatt wasn't. Walton got started with a $25,000 loan from his father-in-law but no family money graced Wyatt. Walton made a great display of his frugality and appetite for work, and expected his people to toil such ridiculously long hours that employee burnout was more or less expected. For a long time, his desk was a piece of plywood. Wyatt, on the other hand, enclosed his people in a beautiful office building as soon as he could afford to build one. To shorten his executives' time on the road he bought several company planes over the years (which he has flown in only three times in his life).

It's no surprise, then, that longevity and loyalty marked his relationships with his employees, not exhaustion. Ann McGee has been with Wyatt for thirty-three years and counting. Ditto Henry Goodwin. Controller Jean Gallman worked for him for twenty years. Carmen Cordero joined the fold in 1986; you can still chat with her at her desk at Sage Valley, but you'd better be quick because she's got bigger fish to fry than jawing about the old days. Wyatt saw potential in Rosa Loyo, a young woman from Barranquitas, Puerto Rico, who was working in housekeeping at Sage Valley in 2001. He gradually increased her responsibility, and now she is his administrative assistant.

As things turned out, despite their cultural differences, something about Wyatt clicked with the folks in Bentonville. Why? The answer is complicated; success has many fathers, as they say, but failure is an orphan. Wyatt had a dedicated staff—headed by his Chief Operating Officer, the rough-and-tough Henry Goodwin—an involved, sympathetic banker, a great builder and even greater timing. The simplest explanation can't be far off: Wyatt worked *very* hard and he had talent. Possibly it came down to a gentle virtue—integrity.

A case in point: the Bluefield, Virginia, Wal-Mart sat two miles from the city water main. So the developer, Wyatt, had a trench dug and pipe laid, a slow and expensive project accomplished in the snow and ice of a brutal winter. The cost would be offset, however, by future fees from anyone who tapped into the line, a possibility Wyatt discussed with Rob Walton, Sam's son. Rob apparently forgot the conversation, but a few years later, a check for $154,000 from the City of Bluefield arrived at Wyatt Development. What do I do with this, asked Jean Gallman, the controller. Send half of it to Wal-Mart, the boss said—they paid for half of that pipe in their rent. Unaccustomed to receiving money out-of-the-blue from its developers, Wal-Mart returned the check. Wyatt sent it back again and in time finally convinced his biggest client that the $77,000 was theirs.

"I pride myself on keepin' my word," was Wyatt's last comment on the subject.

According to Rob Walton, the incident came up the next time the Wal-Mart real-estate committee met to match construction projects with builders. "Give those to Weldon," Walton said. "He's the only honest developer I know."

An *honest* developer...if any profession conjures an

image of double-dealing and taking advantage, it's the developer—that too clever capitalist who finesses grandpa out of his farm in order to put up apartment buildings, parking lots, and a Starbucks. That one of the most famous men in America, Donald Trump, is also a famously obnoxious real-estate developer doesn't help the p.r. But while Trump and Weldon Wyatt are as dissimilar as bagels and beach balls, they're also quite alike in some ways. There's their genius for recognizing the possibilities in land and buildings and businesses, of course. Both admire spit and polish—Trump went to military school—and both have owned and built golf courses. Both are enormously generous in their support of charities. And though their motivations for doing so were one hundred and eighty degrees apart, the flamboyant man from Queens and the modest gentleman from Pacolet have allowed books to be written about them. Which is handy, because in *TRUMP The Art of the Deal*, the Donald and co-author Tony Schwartz outlined the philosophy that has made him such a wonder. Wyatt commented on their applicability to his own point of view.

—Think big, Trump wrote. That's the first thing: "If you're going to be thinking anyway, you might as well think big. Most people think small, because most people are afraid of success, afraid of making decisions, afraid of winning."

Wyatt agreed. "It's just as easy to do things big as to do them small, and obviously, bigger risks mean bigger rewards," he said. "People perceive risk based on what they know. The unknown gives people problems."

But, because of his unusual ability to see through the mist surrounding a potential deal, not much makes Wyatt uncomfortable.

—Focus. Trump referred to his as "almost a controlled neurosis" and "almost maniacal."

Again, Wyatt agreed, but in his own idiom. "It's something you live with seven days a week, twenty-four hours a day"—and then, in expanding his answer, he revealed the mystery behind the bus.

"By not flying, I can keep thinking and keep working. I'm not that out of touch: there's fax and phone [but no computer]. When we drove out to Palm Springs last winter, that was when the bank idea came to me [Wyatt started Savannah River Banking Company in 2007]. I can look out the window and see so many ways to make a living. I love to take a raw piece of dirt and create something...So it's not that I wring my hands and sweat, I just don't enjoy flying."

—Know the market. Trump relies more on his instincts than on data. "I don't hire a lot of number-crunchers," he wrote. "I don't trust fancy marketing surveys." Wyatt—the same.

—TRUMP BELIEVES IN PRESSING HIS ADVANTAGE. WYATT IS NO SHRINKING VIOLET, EITHER—

"When you start listening to numbers guys, not much happens," he said. "There were very, very few deals that Henry [Goodwin] thought I should do. Someone said to him, as smart as you are, why aren't you doing deals? He said 'because Weldon's got bigger balls.'

"Of course, I try to understand the demographics and use common sense. But it doesn't take me long to make a decision, and I'll hire the people who know what I don't know.

"I could always expedite a deal real fast because of the effort I made in maintaining relationships. I have more than an interest in the deal, I have an interest in them. I enjoy knowing about people, what they like and don't like, what makes them tick."

—Leverage. Not surprisingly, Trump believes in pressing any advantage. Wyatt is no shrinking violet, either. Having such a tight relationship with Wal-Mart was certainly a big stick in a discussion with, say, a shoe store shopping for a great location. Wyatt recalled the time a man came to him, virtually insisting that he buy his six-and-a-half acres and a house in Aiken. Wyatt wasn't interested; he doesn't do residential. But the man almost begged. His wife had died, he'd bought another house, he had to sell quickly, and he knew Mr. Wyatt had the means to pay cash. "I'll make you an offer, provided you don't get mad when you hear it," the developer said. "Two hundred thousand." The man took it quite happily.

Then, an inspiration: Wyatt paid the man from son Tom's trust fund.

"Dad, why did you buy that house with my money?" Tom asked.

"So I can prove to you why real estate is better than the stock market," he replied. With a bit of patience, and a small fee, Wyatt had the property re-zoned to multi-family use, and sold it for $350,000. Now, he said to Tom, as he handed him the check, tell me how much you made in the stock market last year.

—Budgets: both Trump and Wyatt believe in containing costs, hardly a revolutionary idea, but it's a concept that's not always easy to apply. "We developed 150 million to 200 million dollars a year for twenty years, and we were never over budget," Wyatt recalls. "Henry did the budgets. He's one of the few people on earth I'd trust with my life. But he doesn't trust anybody."

Wyatt's streak of hitting his projected numbers ended, however, when he built a golf course. "Oh yes, we had a budget," he said. "Then we doubled it."

—Trump trumpets his use of publicity and his willingness to fight as keys to his success. "I don't subscribe to that at all," Wyatt said. "I prefer the Biblical approach to adversaries. I believe in the Golden Rule, that everybody wants to be treated fairly. Now, how do you determine what's fair? Simple: whatever you're willing to pay, you ought to be willing to take.

"It amazes me how money affects business morals. I know a man who lost millions of dollars of future business over seventy thousand dollars."

Faith in God doesn't come up in Trump's book, but Wyatt wants it mentioned in his. Yet he is refreshingly understated about his spiritual life. He draws a straight line between his wealth and success and God's will, but he doesn't hit you over the head with it. There's none of that spurious "gospel of prosperity" stuff you can find on television.

"The three most important people in a person's life are his preacher, his doctor, and his educator," Wyatt says. "Then we get jealous of them or don't want to pay them anything. But you've got to give back. It's required of an individual, and it's the best feeling you can have. A lot of times people forget that what they have isn't really theirs...."

"I don't talk about my religion a lot. I want to live my religion. Hopefully, some people will take that as my testimony."

❧

WELDON

Things went so well in 1984 that Wyatt bought his first plane and his first bus.

He didn't care too much about the King Air prop plane, but the bus was a silver and blue beauty, a forty-foot MCI-9 made by Motor Coach Industries, a major supplier to Greyhound. With that long wheelbase and six big wheels dampening bumps and its Allison 740 four-speed transmission shifting gears in a whisper, Wyatt's bus rode like a magic carpet. His home on wheels had all the doodads and horrible gas mileage you'd expect, and a blank destination box in the roof over the windshield. His driver was an easy-to-be with man named David.

Oh, the places they'd go! David and Wyatt rode the bus all over the Southeast. Once Wyatt got a sort of existential jolt when he realized he was developing a shopping center just a few miles from the seminary in North Carolina his father had attended thirty years before. But most days his thoughts stayed on two tasks, evaluating potential new sites for Wal-Marts and other retailers and checking on the progress of current construction. From time to time a suit from Bentonville would come out to see a proposed location and to compare notes with Wyatt regarding the local economy and population trends. "I remember flying in to look at a site and there'd be Weldon with his motor home," recalls Seay. "If it was late at night, he'd have dinner for us. We sure liked that!"

Wyatt Development had taken an important step forward when Henry Goodwin joined the firm. In the interim between the first Wal-Mart and the second, Wyatt had teamed with a developer on a couple of projects in Myrtle Beach, then hired Goodwin away from his erstwhile partners. Goodwin was several things that Wyatt was not: gruff, direct, and obsessive about the little things. "He was the idea man and I was the detail man," recalls Goodwin, another of those who have stayed in business with Wyatt through decades. "He'd always say, 'I'll catch the bear, you skin it.'

"Basically, Weldon owned the company and I managed it. All the development projects and the day-to-day operation came through my office. He stayed involved but he wasn't much for details." The boss provided a vision, in other words, not a blueprint....

To describe the mid-'80s advance of Wyatt Development, Goodwin uses the word "snowball."

"Let's see," says Allen Woods, the project manager for Gilliam Construction, a company Wyatt used regularly. "Our first Wal-Mart was Barnwell, then Lexington, then a pause, then in '87 and '88, Augusta and North Augusta. And then they came with a vengeance. It wasn't too long before we were building ten a year, in two or three states at a time. We built ten or twelve and then the total was twenty or thirty, then forty or fifty.

"Basically we were building a shell. You heat it, cool it, and paint it, and Wal-Mart puts in the fixtures. Most of them were thirty to fifty thousand square feet, and they were going for fifteen dollars a square foot. They were cheap, I tell you...We had to learn quickly. What we had to find out—and we did find out, partially, on the first one—was that you have to find the right sub-contractors. You can't just go to the local towns and train 'em.

"One time we got bogged down in Bluefield, Virginia. Just snow and ice for two months so bad that we couldn't work. When it thawed out in March, we worked around the clock because we had a June 1 turnover [finish date] and Weldon wouldn't hear of us not meeting the deadline. He's as motivated and aggressive a person as I've ever met. Very positive, very tough, and fair and honest."

Wyatt's burgeoning empire, however, would not have made it to the starting line without the mother's milk of big business: credit. That aspect of his operation rolled as smoothly as his MCI-9, partly because of his characteristically long, loyal relationship with his banker, Norman Tisdale.

Tisdale, like Wyatt the son of a South Carolina mill town—his was Drayton Mills—funded the first big Wyatt Development project in Aiken. And while the name of his employer changed in the familiar big-fish-eating-small-fish cycle—Tisdale worked for August-Kohn, then First National of South Carolina, then South Carolina National, then Wachovia, all without changing jobs—loans to Wyatt remained a constant.

"I was comfortable with Weldon because of our similar backgrounds and because I thought that he always told me the truth," says Tisdale, who personally handled the Wyatt account for twenty years. "He did everything by the book. He bonded [insured] everybody, he had good people working for him, and his buildings were high quality."

Tisdale's bank handled only Wyatt's Wal-Mart deals, which grew in size very quickly after that first one in Aiken. Land fees escalated along with Wal-Mart's and Wyatt's reputations. Wyatt hired surrogates to bid on real estate for him and still had to pay $16 million for one site. The average loan from Tisdale's bank was in the $25-30 million range but went as high as $45 million.

"We were never his only source of money. He bought an inn and a plantation, and a savings and loan financed those," Tisdale recalls. "Money was too easy back then [in the late '80s]. Too loose a money causes problems."

Every May beginning in 1985, the bus rolled west on
I-20 and kept rolling, across endless Texas and the desert South-
west all the way to Sodom and Gomorrah. Wyatt's annual trip to
the International Council of Shopping Center Developers was not
an occasion for fun. Las Vegas—need we even say it?—was not
his style. But he felt he had to go to meet the retailers who would
fill the spaces on the periphery of his solid gold anchor tenant,
Wal-Mart. Weldon and brother Joe and Henry Goodwin had
handshakes and grins for the representatives from Revco, Stein
Mart, Dollar Tree, Dress for Less, Ross, and many others. "I also
met with purchasers," Wyatt says, companies that wanted to
buy the ground and sometimes a building next to a Wal-Mart.
"That was where the real money was." His competitors were on

the glitzy scene in force—the big ones were E. J. DeBartolo and Sons, Developers Diversified, and Cousins. The other guys had elaborate booths on the convention-center floor, with showgirls wearing not much more than a tan and a smile to lure the conventioneers inside. The Wyatt Development booth—need we even say it?—employed no one in fishnets.

"We'd have breakfast at seven, and be in the booth at eight-thirty, and stay there until six," Wyatt recalls. Convention and Vegas protocol then demanded dinner and drinks with a client and then a repeat of the whole thing the day after that, and the next. In a decade or more of going to the big ICSC convention, Wyatt saw exactly one show.

"I hated to go out to dinner, but I did it," Wyatt says. "I'm no drinker. I'm not social."

With her sparkling personality, Brenda could have enjoyed the bright lights that her husband barely tolerated. "No, I didn't go with him to any conventions," she says without apparent regret. "I stayed home and watched the kids, and Weldon knew they were in good hands."

But the Wyatts weren't without fun. Vacation trips to their house at Edisto Island—just north of Parris Island—had by the mid-'80s become part of the family routine. Ashley would bring along three of her friends and Tom three of his for swimming and sand-castle building. Brenda packed her cole slaw grater; Weldon brought some work and an antsy expression. Eventually they reached an accommodation: after a day or two at the beach, Father was allowed to hustle back to the office for

–WHILE HIS GUESTS ENJOYED THEMSELVES, WYATT OBSERVED HIS GUESTS–

a day, a six-hour round trip. Then, replenished, he'd return to the beach to face the difficult task of doing nothing.

But Weldon Wyatt *knows* how to party—his way. He enjoyed his annual bash a lot more than his vacations, partly because the Wyatt Development soiree was relatively brief and mostly because business blended with the pleasure.

"It was a huge, two-day party, with two or three hundred people, usually starting on a Tuesday in September," he recalls. "I invited all the people I dealt with, especially tenants and purchasers." The two or three hundred played golf or tennis at Houndslake, a medium-good country club in Aiken, aimed shotguns at doves in a nearby pasture, and toasted their host. Tuesday meant a big dinner and Casino Night, with head-turning prizes such as Rolex watches and trips to Europe and Hawaii. No one talked turkey, for the most part, but relationships grew stronger, which eased the way to deals down the line. "Because of those parties," Wyatt says, "I never had any trouble getting someone to look at my properties."

While his guests enjoyed themselves, he observed his guests. Wyatt thought it especially useful to tee it up with a potential business partner. "I watched how they marked their ball, and how they reacted to bad breaks," he says. "You play a round of golf with a man, you know more about him than his neighbor of twenty years."

But more than golf and way more than the beach, Wyatt found fulfillment in development. Making something out of nothing—providing a profit for the entrepreneur and employment for the worker—that's what floated Wyatt's boat. Money became less important, he says, than "the thrill of making deals. They used to tease me in the office that the size of a deal didn't matter to me. Which was probably right: getting it done how I wanted it done was my main satisfaction."

But that's only true up to a point. Most of all, Wyatt liked what his creativity did for people he knew and people he'd never meet. "Helping others gives you a wonderful feeling," he says. "It gives me a big high."

ॐ

ASHLEY, WELDON, AND TOM

The go-go '80s rolled to a close. Realizing at age eighteen that when she married she wanted the maiden name of her real daddy, Ashley went through the formal adoption process and became Ashley Wyatt. She also enrolled at Furman, with a major in biology. "Ashley was—is—a very reserved, beautiful girl," says her Aunt Judy, Weldon's sister. "She was very close with Joe's stepdaughter."

Judy also has a ready description of her nephew: "Tom is Joe Wyatt up one side and down the other. He can crack you up in a skinny minute."

Tom inherited Uncle Joe's sense of humor and his skill in golf. Under the tutelage of Jackie Seawell at Woodside Plantation in Aiken, Tom became one of the best junior golfers in the state. And Brenda became a golf mom, taking her son to tournaments, and when the time came, driving his high-school teams to their matches. Watching proudly with her was her father, Hastings Grice. The best butcher in Aiken had gotten his grandson started in the game with his first set of sawed off clubs.

"Dad made my tournaments when he could," says Tom, evincing no regret that, usually, Dad couldn't. "He's always done everything he could to make my life easier. He's helped me when I needed it and when I didn't know I needed it. You couldn't ask for a better father."

(And then Tom the jokester has to laugh. "What I just said to you was my exact toast to my Dad when Leslie and I got married.")

Humility was the byword at home. The kids knew the family had money, but with their father quoting his father regarding putting pants on one leg at a time, and their mother not having it in her to put on airs, Ashley and Tom were grounded, polite, and easy to like. All was well with the Wyatts.

Then trouble arrived in the blink of an eye. Weldon Wyatt was like a boxer handling an inferior opponent with ease, when suddenly the other guy lands a sharp jab, a hook to the ribs, and a knockout punch.

WELDON AND TOM

Chapter 5

IF YOU GIVE ME TIME

If you can dream and not make dreams your master

If you can think and not make thought your aim

If you can meet with Triumph and Disaster

And treat those two impostors just the same…

—"If" by Rudyard Kipling

The two office buildings Wyatt built on Silver Bluff Road in Aiken would not look out of place in upscale, high tech Atlanta. Constructed of cast concrete painted beige and brown with green accents, the two two-story buildings are identical and side-by-side. Their front doors are at right angles to the street, and are connected by a walkway sheltered by crape myrtles that bloomed bright red in the summer. A fountain at the midway point is a natural spot for those on a coffee, cigarette, or lunch break, and the splashing water provides a soothing sound track. One of the handsome structures housed the seventy-five employees of Wyatt Development and the other was leased.

WELDON AND JOE

Wyatt could have walked to work from his house at Woodside Plantation. His entire family lived not much farther away. All of them were not just close physically, but also tight emotionally. Dennis would have a drink at Joe's house, Judy would drop in for coffee at Weldon's, and they all ate dinner, from time to time, with Hayden and Estoy. But on one typical, casual visit of one sibling with another, on August 22, 1991, Joe fell dead in Judy's house. Heart attack. He was forty-six.

"Right over there," says Judy Wyatt Parker, gesturing from a chair in her home office, unable to suppress her tears. Her brother lived three doors down on their lovely street, and he'd just stopped in to say hello. "Joe inspired us," Judy says. "Losing him was the most traumatic thing that ever happened to us.... So sad."

Joe's death shocked everyone in the family. Tom remembers a wonderful uncle who looked like his father yet was so unlike him. "The perfect entertainer," he says. "A barrel of laughs. And an amazing golfer, really a good talent."

Weldon had lost a brother and a sparkling presence in his office. "I was very devastated," he says. "I was six years older. I'd helped raise him."

Joe Dan White came down from Chattanooga for the funeral. Wyatt's best friend from Pacolet couldn't help but recall during the service that Weldon's little brother had been named for him. White approached Wyatt after the service, shook his hand, and looked into his eyes. "You're going to be all right, Weldon," he said. Wyatt, drawn but dry-eyed, nodded and said, "I know."

Considering the reversals he'd suffered in the previous seventeen months, his confidence—if that's what is was—was impressive. Twice Wyatt had been pummeled to the ground by events more or less out of his control.

First and worst was something called the savings and loan crisis. S & Ls—the junior varsity of banking—were in trouble throughout the '80s. Mortgage borrowing in the United States had boomed from $700 billion in 1976 to $1.2 trillion in 1980, and interest rates were very high, which should have been a formula for success for the S & Ls. It wasn't. Burdened by low-interest loans on their books and low-interest rates that attracted few depositors, the "thrifts," as they were called, were barely scraping by. Congress and the Reagan Administration deregulated the S & L industry, a well intentioned loosening of the rules that turned a problem into the worst economic disaster since the Depression.

Among the many bad ideas passed into law in the name of S & L reform was that of raising deposit insurance—a federal guarantee to repay—from $40,000 per account to $100,000. This pen stroke caused S & Ls to take greater and greater risks and to invest in ventures they weren't qualified to assess. In this fast-changing, loophole-filled world,

—"WELDON LOOKED HORRIBLE, LIKE A GHOST, " MCGEE SAYS, "HE'D BEEN WORRYING, AND HE'S NOT A WORRIER."—

crooks, cynics and scoundrels tried to get rich the old-fashioned way, by cheating the government.

Wyatt, unfortunately, had a financial partner in Dayton Associates. "The guys from Ohio," as they were known around the office, owned twenty percent of a large number of

Wyatt developments. Dayton's money was borrowed from S & Ls all over the country. When the S & Ls failed, Dayton failed, and Wyatt Development teetered on the edge. It was as if they were all tied with same rope.

One morning in February 1990, Wyatt was told he was underwater. Underwater means broke. He needed $32 million to get even.

"The day the bottom fell out with these guys from Dayton, Weldon looked horrible, like a ghost," recalls his secretary, Ann McGee. "He'd been worrying, and he's not a worrier. He tried to keep the problems to himself for a while, but I knew something was wrong.

"He called a meeting in the conference room. It got emotional." The hugs and tears made the boss "very uncomfortable," says McGee. Wyatt's not a hugger.

He struggled to control the uncontrollable situation. He laid off all but a handful of his seventy-five employees. He called Brenda; then he called a real-estate agent. As fast as they could, the Wyatts sold their house, their cars, and the beach house, and moved into a three-bedroom condo. Ashley offered to transfer from Furman to a less expensive public school, but her parents told her to stay put.

"Bleak," is Henry Goodwin's one-word assessment of this period. "Massive lay-offs and salary reductions....The guys in Ohio did some fraudulent things, and the banks took over....We held on because we had enough fees from property management coming in to keep the lights on."

The $285 *billion* S & L meltdown put other real estate developers in the same fix. Many—if not most—declared bankruptcy. Despite pressure from various lawyers and accountants,

Wyatt would not. "That's because of the way I was raised," he says. "I told the banks, 'if you give me time, I'll pay you.'"

But there was no time. Bankruptcy was the only option. A date was set to sign the papers. A little money trickled in, and the date was pushed forward. Again. And again…six times the surrender was postponed. Meanwhile, the experts reminded Wyatt that he'd be at least $25 million ahead if he'd repudiate the debt and just sign on the line.

The holidays arrived, somberly, and with unusually cold temperatures. On Christmas Eve, Wyatt's phone rang. Sir, someone from the Aiken fire department said, you'd better get down to your office. Your pipes have burst. Your office is flooded.

"All our records were destroyed," says Ann McGee with a sigh. "It was devastating."

Judy recalls her brother in the midst of the sodden mess. For the only time in her life, she saw him cry.

The completion of the problematic Wal-Mart in Blue-field, Virginia, marked an important milestone in Wyatt Development's comeback. Joe's death a few months later sank Wyatt into sadness again, but not into gloom. His determination would not permit depression.

And a number of good things resulted from the personal and professional ordeals. He bought back most of his properties, for one thing, and at a thirty percent discount. "We gained a lot of credibility with lenders because we didn't fold our tents," Wyatt says. Indeed, banks competed avidly for business from the man who honored his debts no matter what—although Norman Tisdale kept the lion's share.

"The message I got out of it was if you do the right thing, you're better off," Wyatt says.

"I changed my lifestyle. Sometimes when you have a little success, you need something to bring you back to reality. I'd gotten too big for my shoes...I became less of a risk taker. In business and spiritually, I changed."

For Wyatt, one incident crystallized the short shrift he'd been giving his faith: he'd been eyeing a piece of Aiken real estate with the idea of buying it for his church, which he did, but before he could give it away, someone offered a very good price for it, and he accepted. It bothered him for months that he hadn't followed through on this plan known only to himself. After an unlikely series of events allowed him to reacquire the land, he promptly donated it to Town Creek Baptist.

"There were so many moving pieces, so many tentacles in that deal—and from being about $38 million in the hole to $50 or 60 million ahead in just a few years—I thought God had to be involved," Wyatt says.

He tithed—a ten percent donation to the church is a considerable sum when you make many millions a year—and his charitable giving accelerated. Much of it was and remains invisible; he doesn't want to talk about how much he gives away and to whom. But here's an act of kindness he doesn't know I know: Wyatt heard of an Aiken high school that was embarrassed by an almost total lack of seating for spectators at its football field. A short time before the school's Big Game, motivated workmen erected aluminum bleachers that could seat a thousand people, a sight so magnificent that some of the football players cried when they saw it. The donor remained anonymous.... If a worthy cause involves children, athletics, education, or the Baptist church, Weldon Wyatt's a soft touch.

WELDON AND BRENDA 1997

"He became more loving—not that he wasn't before," says Ashley. "And he enjoyed his family more—not that he hadn't before."

Ashley got married to JD Donaldson In 1997 at Aiken First Baptist, and the Wyatts became friends with the pastor, the profound and humorous Fred Andrea. A few years later, they joined his flock. Andrea agrees in a mellow baritone that Weldon has a wonderful ability to evaluate a business deal. "But I don't think his insight is limited to real estate," Andrea says. "It's his perspective on life, on existence, and his relationships with others. To understand his philosophy you have to understand his theology. He has the ability to see clearly, and deeply, and intuitively.

"Sorry, I tend to think and speak in threes."

In 1999, Wyatt was diagnosed with prostate cancer. He and Brenda rode in the bus up to Johns Hopkins in Baltimore. Ashley and Tom—and Ashley's husband JD—flew up in the company jet. Everyone prayed, and he made it out OK.

In 2001, Wyatt sold everything but one shopping center.

He didn't retire.

CHAPTER 6

SAGE VALLEY

CLIFF ROBERTS AND BOBBY JONES SET THE BAR. AND WE TRY
TO GO OVER IT, NOT UNDER IT. I DON'T KNOW ANY CLUB THAT
DOES WHAT WE DO AT THE LEVEL WE DO....

THE NEAT THING IS—WHERE ELSE IN THE WORLD CAN YOU
FIND TWO GOLF COURSES LIKE AUGUSTA NATIONAL AND
SAGE VALLEY, ONLY FIFTEEN MINUTES APART?

—WELDON WYATT

That steak was so big last night that I couldn't finish it. And then I found myself eating that cake. But it was so good...

Walking up here this morning with that dew on the ground and the sun coming up, it was so pretty...

I'll have three egg whites, some fruit, black coffee... OK, one piece of bacon...OK, just give me eggs Benedict.

—Sage Valley guests at breakfast, May 2007

Just as shifting tectonic plates cause an earthquake, several very large things had to move to enable the creation of Sage Valley. It's difficult to rank their importance, or in some cases, even their chronological order. In the end, Wyatt would be four ways like—of all people—Willie Nelson. Don't laugh: both cruise in luxury tour buses; despite the severest inducements to do so, neither would declare bankruptcy (Willie, you'll recall, sold everything and made an album—"The IRS Tapes"—to square his $16.7 million debt to the federal government); both think of charity as their highest calling; and both own and operate very private golf courses. Willie and Weldon will have lots to talk about if they ever meet.

In a way, Sage Valley began the day Tom Wyatt said, "Dad, have you got a minute?" In the aftermath of the cancer scare in 1999, when everyone in the family mulled the enormous implications of mortality, Tom, then a junior at Furman, told his father he did not want to take over the family business.

Although Wyatt says "I was building the company for my son," he also claims to have been neither surprised nor disappointed at Tom's decision. "No, no regrets about that," he says. "Tom would have had nowhere to go but down." Besides, being a Wal-Mart developer had changed a lot. The retailer's continued explosive growth had reduced the fun and increased the pressure, and, as the decade wore on, all the old guard Wyatt had enjoyed working with in Bentonville had quit or retired.

Sage Valley © Thom Abbott Golf Collection 2007

TOM AND WELDON IN THE CLUBHOUSE

"Wal-Mart didn't want me to stop," Wyatt says. "They were very good to me, but I don't miss it. The best part of my day is waking up and not caring what Wal-Mart thinks."

As his interest in Wal-Mart waned, Wyatt's business brain turned to investments in golf. With several partners, he bought Houndslake in Aiken—it was in dire financial straits, and he played golf and cards there already—then Jones Creek in Augusta. This new direction definitely interested Tom, a member of the Furman golf team. Given his father's lifelong pattern of doing

Sage Valley © Thom Abbott Golf Collection 2007

everything possible to control his surroundings—the bus, his business life—Tom was not surprised that his father started talking about having his own place. As usual, the distance between thought and action was very short.

Why golf? Wyatt loves the game, to start with, particularly its history and the purity of the competition ingrained in it. "It's self discipline," Wyatt says. "You're your own judge and referee. It's life skills."

SAGE VALLEY COTTAGES
FACING THE PRACTICE
HOLES

THE CLUBHOUSE OCCUPIES
HIGH GROUND ABOVE
THE GOLF COURSE AND THE
THREE PRACTICE HOLES

But his decision to consider golf as an investment had less to do with the game's homely virtues than with the success of the parties he'd staged at Houndslake. He thought about expanding the concept: what if he built a golf course that was intriguing and not merely good; with food that was heavenly and not merely palatable; and an atmosphere that whispered luxury and privacy, with no views of highways or gas stations? What if Club Wyatt did every little thing as well as it could possibly be

Sage Valley © Thom Abbott Golf Collection 2007

done? In theory, such a club would attract a national membership of wealthy businessmen setting up deals with a capital D. It would be a little like that nearby playground in the pines where the members wear green jackets.

And, speaking of the home of the Masters: as Wyatt began this new venture, the whispers started. Were they true? Had he been invited to join Augusta National, would the idea of Sage Valley have even occurred to him? Did he build his own club in retaliation?

In a word, no. "Anyone who's fooled with golf would like to be a member at the National," says Wyatt, who has played Augusta National at least fifty times. "But building Sage Valley had nothing to do with that. I just wanted to create something great in golf." Wyatt doesn't mention that one of his best friends and his frequent host was the late

Jackson Stephens, a very popular chairman of Augusta National. You have the sense that if they'd wanted to push it, Wyatt could have gotten in.

Whatever the relationship of Sage Valley to Augusta National was to be, the home of the Masters had an impossible-to-duplicate cachet. But Sage Valley would have something unique, too. Although Wyatt didn't think of it right away, his club wouldn't be just great golf and fine dining. "If you've read much about Bobby Jones, you know that when he came here (to the Augusta area, in the '20s through the '40s, until he became ill) he'd play golf for a couple of days, then hunt quail in Waynesboro for a couple of days. Golf and bird hunting kind of go together, particularly in the South.

"Ever been to Thomasville or Albany, Georgia, in November? During bird season, the little airport there is just clogged with five hundred private jets. Golf is a $25 billion industry. Hunting is a *$75* billion industry."

While Sage Valley was still on his mental drawing board, Wyatt's dream course leaped dramatically forward when he hired the perfect right-hand man. Dave Christensen wasn't easy to get. On his way to building a national reputation in the club management business, Christensen's colorful career ascended from the Ramada Inn in Aiken; to a degree from the Culinary Institute of America in New York, immediately after high school; to a sous-chef post at Fripp Island, South Carolina; to owning and operating his own restaurant, Fireside Deli, in Aiken; and then to two years as a chef instructor at the Greenbriar, the four-star resort in Virginia. From chef, Christensen shifted smoothly into greater responsibility with Club Corporation of America—by far the world's largest club management company—where he was the youngest manager in the company's history. After several stops at CCA-run clubs in Texas, Christensen's circle finally looped back to Woodside Plantation in Aiken, his hometown. Twice on his watch, Woodside was named CCA's Club of the Year, and he was pronounced Manager of the Year. He'd always been willing to move to learn something new or to experience a different culture, but after twenty-two years with CCA, he was back in his hometown, and he had a wife and a child and security.

Three times Christensen turned down Wyatt's offer to run a club that didn't yet exist. Finally, in October 2000, he accepted. His office would be a trailer in the middle of nowhere, but grander things awaited.

The final piece that energized the whole was Tom. As his graduation from Furman approached—he got a BA in History in 2001—his attitude changed about where to live and work post-college. "I think when you're a kid, you can't wait to get out of your hometown," he says. "But then I knew I wanted to come back to Aiken." His father's quickly coalescing plan to build an elite golf club drew him home and turned him on the way no Wal-Mart development ever could. What role would you like me to play? Tom asked his father, who, seeing the depth of his son's passion for the project, made him co-owner and Club President.

Where would you build, Tom asked (by the summer of 2000, Wyatt knew exactly where the course would go). And—a big question, since it carves in stone a golf course's identity—whom would they hire to design it? Both Weldon and Tom admired Donald Ross, the sainted Scotsman who designed, among others, Palmetto and Pinehurst #2. Of modern architects, both loved the work of golf's perfect gentleman, Ben Crenshaw, who, with his partner, Bill Coore, creates courses that salute the dead masters yet say something new.

But how would they choose an architect? And how would they know the best elements of the best clubs? Weldon Wyatt answered these questions the way he always did: he got on his bus and had a look for himself.

୭୬

Sage Valley © Thom Abbott Golf Collection 2007

WELDON AND TOM

It's interesting to observe how the patterns of a lifetime repeated themselves as Wyatt sharpened his vision of the perfect club. He focused on his new development all day, every day, like an actor on a role. He controlled everything but was willing to delegate anything. As always, he relied on his own judgment regarding the market—not on an expert, and certainly not on data from a computer. And he risked a lot for a potential big reward. He rolled the dice on the land, that's for sure.

Wyatt had located some wonderful golf terrain right in his own back yard, in Graniteville, the old mill town he knew so well from his childhood. The owner, Prudential Timber, had a vast tract of gorgeous rolling ground with plenty of trees even after it had been harvested for lumber. Wyatt bought five hundred acres. Golf courses require less than half that, but for privacy purposes, Wyatt thought it wise to have a bit of cushion from whatever might spring up on the other side of his fence. Two years later, he purchased another nine hundred acres to wrap around the five hundred, just making extra certain there'd be no views of a Waffle House. At the real estate closing, the timber company asked if he'd be interested in its entire parcel, another 8800 acres, for $18 million. Yes, Wyatt said.

—"I TOLD WELDON WHAT HE HAD IN MIND WASN'T REALLY FEASIBLE," FAZIO SAYS. "THE INCOME VERSUS THE EXPENSE WAS WAY OUT OF BALANCE."—

"But I had no idea what I'd do with that land," he says. He would not, could not, stick a housing development on it, because that would contradict the entire point of the luxurious retreat he pictured. A little later, the idea of the hunting preserve came into his head like the ding of the timer on a stove.

With land in hand, Wyatt and Son hit the road. They examined the work of classic—that is, deceased—architects at Cypress Point and Pebble Beach on the rock- bound coast of Carmel, California. They marveled at the stark, almost lunar beauty of Coore/Crenshaw's design at the Sand Hills in Mullen, Nebraska. Iron Horse, in Whitefish, Montana, had incredible mountain views and wonderful architecture from Tom Fazio. Pete Dye's design of The Honors Course in Ooltewah, near Chattanooga, showed off his amazing artistry. One measure of the

Sage Valley © Thom Abbott Golf Collection 2007

Wyatts' enthusiasm—or something—is shown by the timing of
their visit to Double Eagle, the Tom Weiskopf and Jay Morrish
course near Columbus, Ohio: after a couple of days of golf and
fine dining, their forty-five-foot Featherlite bus rolled to Johns
Hopkins in Baltimore for Weldon's cancer surgery.

The Wyatts noticed shadings and subtleties in the great
courses too numerous to mention, but one of their similarities
would be key to Sage Valley. All the great courses Wyatt got to

know and one he knew already—Augusta National—had bent grass greens. So he wanted bent grass greens. Bent just *hates* hot weather, however, which is part of the reason the National closes its gates from May through September. But Wyatt was determined not to have any lengthy shutdown. Bent, South Carolina summer heat, no shutdown…this would be a major hurdle.

Wyatt loved the playability of Double Eagle and got to be good friends with its owner, John H. McConnell. But he'd been

Sage Valley © Thom Abbott Golf Collection 2007

predisposed to Crenshaw and Coore, and Sand Hills had blown him away. So he called the two-time Masters champion at his office in Austin. Bill flew in and toured the site and listened to the thoughts of the owner. Ultimately, however, the Texans felt their minimalist style did not mesh with what Wyatt required. Utilizing the existing terrain is Crenshaw/Coore's mantra, and it looked to them that they'd have to move a lot of dirt to get the course Wyatt had in mind. So they recommended he call Tom Fazio.

What a fallback position! No architect has more top one hundred golf courses, so, in that important respect, Fazio is number one in the world. He is also an articulate man with the confidence to speak very plainly about himself and his industry. They met for lunch at Houndslake, and Fazio interviewed Wyatt as much as Wyatt interviewed Fazio.

"Weldon had this vision to create a great golf club, and it's my job to fulfill the owner's dream," says Fazio. "But I'm also a realist. I don't waste a lot of time. I ask a lot of questions, such as how much can you get for a membership for a club in Aiken, South Carolina, and how many members will you need, that sort of thing.

"I told Weldon that what he wanted wasn't really feasible. The potential income versus the expense was way out of balance. But he said, 'I can handle the financial part if you can handle the golf side.'"

So: an owner with money. It was a great start.

Nine times out of ten—maybe more—golf architects must shoehorn their courses into a land plan that emphasizes building lots with golf-course views. Compromises must be made;

holes are often designed with the land *off* the course in mind, because real estate sales are so crucial. But when Fazio saw the site and listened to the owner, he realized he was about to be involved in something rare: "Sage Valley was the ideal situation for an architect: unlimited land, a free hand, and no residential land uses."

SAGE VALLEY ENTRANCE

In Fazio's experience, pine forests and sandy soil always remind potential golf course owners of the timeless results achieved by Donald Ross at Pinehurst. The name came up in Wyatt's discussions with his architect, "but if Wyatt was looking for a particular style, I would have talked him out of it," Fazio says. "There's nothing wrong with Cypress Point, Pebble Beach, and Augusta National, but I approach golf-course design like a writer with a book. Each one should be custom-crafted, unique, one of a kind. When golfers tell me that one of my holes reminds them of something or somewhere else, I shudder. I think: 'I've failed.'"

Fazio signed on. The design and construction of Sage Valley was "fun and exciting," he says. "Not one day of difficulty. But to say it was easy takes away from the commitment a lot of people had to the project."

Virtually unlimited rolling terrain with easily shaped sandy soil: it was, as Fazio said, a dream job. The only real challenge lay in the bent-grass greens. For years now, golf courses have installed giant fans to keep cooling air moving over the fine-bladed northern grass during hot summers. It helps. But a company called Sub Air had a better way. Its systems of underground pipes and pumps regulate the temperature and the moisture of the earth above it. Sub Air is perfect for baseball and football fields, and it is under more than a few—the Philadelphia Phillies and Denver Broncos play on, or above, Sub Air—but the company's most famous installation had been beneath the problematic twelfth green at Augusta National. With the flick of a switch, an operator can warm the green to gently melt frost, cool it on a steamy summer day, or suck excess moisture from rain or irrigation (while water obviously lowers the ground

Sage Valley © Thom Abbott Golf Collection 2007

temperature, which is good, standing water results in shallow roots. To mow bent grass low so it putts fast and true, roots must be strong and growing down). It sounds silly, but it has meaning in golf circles: Sub Air is the Official Subsurface Mechanical Drainage Sytem of the Tournament Players Clubs.

Given his goal of staying open almost year-round and his iron-clad promise to make this thing first class, Wyatt signed off on using Sub-Air's underground vaults and web of pipes for all his greens (and, as it turned out, two of his tees, the seventeenth and the eighteenth.). *Then he bought the company.* Sub Air's world headquarters now sits on a hill a quarter of a mile from the Sage Valley entrance.

Meanwhile, like a pharaoh directing the erection of

Sage Valley © Thom Abbott Golf Collection 2007

pyramids, Dave Christensen handled a thousand details. Club-house and cottage construction, pots and pans, knives and forks, tables and chairs, landscaping, membership, roads, staffing—it's exhausting even to imagine what the former chef prepared and served. And on deadline: Wyatt wanted to open in half a year or less.

Let's consider just one aspect of the General Manager's task: housing. Inside the interior gates would be six residences— a few with four bedrooms, a couple with six, and one massive ten-bedroom dwelling with an exercise room, a spa, and fourteen thousand square feet that strains the word "cottage," the preferred term at Sage Valley. Ten more cottages sit in a clearing in the pines outside the inner gate. To be sure, Wyatt knew the buttons to push on this aspect of the project. On all of it, he and Christensen worked in harness and apparent harmony. And for *lots* of hours. They operate the same informal way, a style Christensen calls "management by walking around."

"I could picture just the way I wanted it to be," Wyatt recalls. And what he didn't want it to be. "I don't know why they [other great golf clubs] have to act so snooty. The upper-income bracket ought to be as common as anyone. Some places pride themselves on being unfriendly. Cliff Roberts probably led the way on this—I think he scared people into behaving. But anybody would be comfortable around Jack Stephens (one of Roberts's successors as chairman at Augusta National.).

"I wanted to make a club where you feel at home, not like you're walking on egg shells. So the two biggest things we planned to do differently are friendliness and caddies. A lot of clubs have caddies but don't put too much emphasis on them. But that caddie can save a fifteen to eighteen handicap player three or four shots a round. The caddie is the most important person here."

Wyatt's tour of great courses led to two other policies: no cell phones—an obvious modern annoyance with no place in an atmosphere where people are trying to relax—and no tipping. "Tipping gets to be a hassle," says Wyatt. "Who do you tip? How much? Where do you stop? The only tip we allow is to caddies and the maximum is forty dollars. If we find a caddie asking for more, he's gone."

With philosophies and facilities in place, and to cut a very involved story short, Opening Day arrived in the fall of 2001. The fully grassed golf course looked magnificent. For the first time, Superintendent Chuck Green cut holes in the greens. Weldon Wyatt would hit the first shot from the first tee, and Tom the second, and their shots were almost guaranteed to look grand hanging in the sky on the dramatically downhill par four. Then, disaster. Violent cowards crashed highjacked passenger jets into the World Trade Center and the Pentagon. Like everyone the world over, the people at Sage Valley stared helplessly at television screens. The last thing anyone wanted was a celebration. Finally, because they had to, the Wyatts played nine holes. Weldon's first tee shot hit the middle of the fairway, his eight-iron second found the middle of the green, and he two-putted for par.

The golf grapevine spread the word: there was something new and special in Graniteville, South Carolina. Wyatt told the *Augusta Chronicle* about his thorough research into golf's best courses. His final eight-stop odyssey confirmed that he already knew the ingredients he wanted in his own club; the only upgrade he discovered was posting the name of the security guard on duty for all to see. "What I've been after since I started this," Wyatt said, "was for our members to come through the gate and say 'wow.' And, most important, when they go out, I want them to say 'wow' again."

Although ranking golf courses is as impossible and subjective as ranking works of art or pretty girls, Top Fifty, Top One Hundred, and Best Of lists have become well established and self-sustaining in the golf industry. But whether you believe them or not, Sage Valley's rankings were incredibly good. *Golf Digest* looked at one hundred and seventy new private courses around the world in 2002 and declared Sage Valley to be seventh best. Later, *Golf Digest* rated America's Fifty Greatest Golf Retreats and named the still brand new Sage Valley number six—in the process naming Augusta National's caddies the best in the country, an assertion that undermined the whole, but still—sixth!

Greater shocks awaited: in *GOLF Magazine*'s eagerly watched America's Greatest One Hundred Courses, Sage Valley debuted at number seventy-eight in 2005, and stayed in the mix in 2007 at number ninety-one, despite hosting only one atten-tion-drawing tournament, the World Club Championship in November 2006. For such a new club, these rankings were spectacular.

"THE CLUB IS KNOWN AS MUCH FOR FOOD AS GOLF," WROTE *GOLF DIGEST*.

"The club is known as much for food as golf," wrote *Golf Digest*. "If a member re-quests Dover sole for dinner, Sage Valley will fly it in."

In another story, *Golf Digest* em-phasized the Sage Valley wine list, and the man responsible for it, Frank Carpenter. As the wine steward at Augusta National, Carpenter had been responsible for compiling one of the best wine collections in the world. The National's cel-lar contained at least 10,000 bottles worth in the millions. Som-melier Carpenter retired; Wyatt coaxed him out of retirement. With his worldwide contacts, the dignified Carpenter was able to acquire some great grape juice, including six vintages of Lafitte Rothschild from as far back as 1975. The Sage Valley house wine would be a tasty blend of Bourdeaux varietals christened Carpenter's Reserve. *Golf Digest's* oenophile was impressed that the club charges only $600 for bottles that sell for over a thousand elsewhere.

Flying in Dover sole…Bourdeaux varietals…six hundred bucks to savor a subtle, fleeting feeling on the tongue…although Wyatt's personal taste in food and drink is light years away from such luxury, he recognized that others, in some circumstances, require it. He always knows his market.

Sage Valley © Thom Abbott Golf Collection 2007

Architects sketch. They watch—sometimes—as bulldozers turn over dirt. And then they're gone. The superintendent's relationship with the golf course is much more intimate and ongoing and just as important. Chuck Green is the man at Sage Valley. Like Christensen, Green, a native of Lake City, South Carolina, has the talent and reputation to work almost anywhere.

"I told them they'd have to move the green," Green is saying. "I cannot grow grass there. You can build some great stuff but when it turns brown, it's not so great."

The superintendent has stopped his work cart in the sixth fairway. As he gestures toward the woods where the green used to be, his dog, Chloe, a black and white Border Collie, hops down to investigate smells mere humans cannot detect. In the tray in the cart is a can of Zodiac dippin' tobacco, a rolled up blueprint, keys, pens, and a blue plastic bottle of 30 SPF sunscreen.

Chloe bounds back into the cart in response to her master's low whistle, and we're off again. We examine tees: "this grass is Eagle Tif-Dwarf. It's a little showy, and it's so tight some members are afraid to take a divot. I heard a guest say, 'hell, our greens aren't this fast." We look at sand: "Some like it fluffy, like Weldon, and some prefer firm, like Tom. Bunkers are the toughest thing for a superintendent." We consider cart paths—which doesn't take long because Sage Valley doesn't really have any. The thinking is that concrete runways ruin the look of a course and interfere with the play. And the traffic will always be so light here that they're probably not needed anyway.

Green, who helped build a course on his father's land when he was six years old, knows everything worth knowing about the several hundred acres he maintains. He knows that it's five to seven degrees cooler here, on average, than in Augusta and Aiken. Part of it's the elevation—about 420 feet above sea level at the highest point. Green knows every arcane fact about soil and grass and pesticide and drainage. He knows how to play the game, too, having been a member of the golf team at Francis Marion University.

"He's definitely detail-oriented," Green says of his owner. "He'll call me about a limb that needs to be trimmed or a pine cone or a cup or a bottle in a creek. He's made me better."

We talk about the brutally hot summer of 2007 as we speed along through sunshine and shadow, and about Green's

Sage Valley © Thom Abbott Golf Collection 2007

favorite hole, the eleventh. It's a dreamy interval: the pines bordering the fairways are towering pillars that diffuse the light on the even green fairways, and the orange pine straw beneath the trees contrasts beautifully. But you've seen all this—that is, if you've ever turned on your TV in April. The resemblance between Sage Valley and Augusta National cannot be missed.

But you've never seen anything like that other part of Sage Valley, the Hunt Club.

With Wyatt's words burned into his brain—"I want mule drawn wagons, a log cabin lodge, and in five years I want us to be as known for hunting as for golf"—Dave Christensen went to work. He decided to tackle the most mysterious aspect of his assignment first. So he went online and found an organization called Mules and More.

"This nice lady on the phone said, 'Why don't you come up to North Carolina next month for our annual Mule Show and Coon Jump,'" Christensen recalls. "Mule Show I could understand, but *Coon Jump*? And when she asked me if I was interested in pack mules, riding mules, wagon mules or jumping mules, I realized I was in over my head. So I did what Mr. Wyatt does: I hired an expert."

The expert was Jack Miller from Thomasville, Georgia, the Quail Hunting Capital of the World. Miller secured all of Sage Valley's mule and horse business with his promise to replace any under-performing animal. And he explained what a coon jump is: some mules have the amusing and possibly useful ability to jump over various heights of split rail fence from a seated position. Don't send me any of those, Christensen said.

Sage Valley Hunt Club wound up with, among others, Kit and Kate. They're Belgian draft mules, massive, impassive animals weighing almost a ton each. Jeff Colley has hitched this pair to one of the hunt club's custom wagons for an early September quail hunting dress rehearsal—the season opens in two weeks.

"Step-up," Colley says in a conversational tone, and the mules pull us out of the immaculate, airy stable.

Quail hunting the Sage Valley way requires quite a crew. Colley, Kit, and Kate guide a wagon loaded, usually, with four hunters, who ride like kings eight feet above the rough trail. On carpeted perches on either side of the driver sit Hambone and Roo-Roo, flushing/retreiving dogs. Pointers—four of them, I think—sniff the exciting air from cages in the belly of the wagon. They'll

RUSS PADGETT, WELDON AND SAGE VALLEY WILDLIFE MANAGER BRAD HARMON

replace the pointers on the ground when they get too hot. At a shouted command from Daryl Thomas, the dog handler, the hunt begins. Thomas; his son, Junior; and Sage Valley biologist Brad Harmon ride on horseback ahead of the cart.

Through thick growths of mature pines, blue stem, broom straw and Indian grass, the pointers sniff and run with obvious joy. Thomas yells commands. Colley follows, saying "gee" and "yaw" (left and right) to the mules and telling brief anecdotes about bird hunting, Texas (where he's from), quarter horses (which he's raised) and Sage Valley. "Dick Cheney was here two weeks before he shot that man in the face," Daryl says. "He's was a very aggressive hunter." Hambone and Roo-Roo quiver, so badly do they want to take part in finding birds. Finally, the pointers freeze—"lock up" in the vernacular— their tails forming exclamation points. If this was an actual hunt, at this point two hunters would climb down from the wagon and load their shotguns with red Winchester Super Target shells. "Roo!" shouts Thomas, and the yellow lab jumps down, to run in tight circles until a quail explodes off the ground. Roo has such a good sniffer, and such stealth, that on one occasion he returns to the wagon with a quail in his mouth. The little brown bird is soggy but unharmed. The happy dog gives it to Colley and sits back down.

The sporting press gave raves to the new hunting paradise in Graniteville. For example:

"A few weeks ago I was checking on a dove field that must represent the crème de la crème of dove fields. It was a 115-acre field planted in sunflower, corn, and wheat. The wheat will mature in early summer and will be mowed a little at a time in order to give the birds plenty of fresh grain throughout the summer. The field has two power lines—one of which was erected just for the doves.

AUTHOR TAKING NOTES WHILE TALKING WITH DAVE CHRISTENSEN

The hunters are brought into the field in a wagon and are dropped off at numbered stands, each of which has a cooler stocked with bottled water, soft drinks, and plenty of ice. A camo umbrella provides relief from the scorching sun.

At the end of the day, hunters are picked up via golf carts and wagons and are transported back to the main hunting lodge for the finest in food, drink, and entertainment. Gourmet chefs prepare the doves and other Southern delights. The day ends with the hunters picking up their processed birds from the cleaning room. It will be the best of days for the hunters included in the event.

"The location is Sage Valley Golf Club, one of the finest and most prestigious golf clubs in the country."

At the center of the Sage Valley hunting experience is the lodge, one of the most incredible buildings I've ever seen.

The hand-hewn log building has a mountaintop feel. It sits on a ridge with a commanding view of the rolling countryside, and in the fall the colors induce a dreamy feeling. Further along the ridge is the skeet shooting and sporting clay facility. It's world class.

The lodge is as big and airy as a church inside, and inspires the same awe you might feel in a cathedral. I sat there on a leather couch, my feet on an Indian rug, the air lit by three massive chandeliers made from antlers. And my eyes traveled up

Sage Valley © Thom Abbott Golf Collection 2007

DAVID ABEL, WELDON WYATT, TOM WYATT, AND KELLY MILLER
AT THE WORLD CLUB CHAMPIONSHIP AT SAGE VALLEY NOVEMBER 2006

above a fireplace big enough to stand in to the top of the monumental, two-story chimney. They built the chimney first, says Dave Christensen, and then enclosed it with a lot of tall pines from the Sage Valley grounds. The fireplace stone is from Tennessee.

"I designed this with Mr. Tucker, from Charleston, and a company from Washington state that specializes in log cabin homes" Christensen says. "Gator Cochrane did all the wrought-iron railings. Mack Millen did all the milling, and he gave us that huge piece of cypress for the mantel. The floors are heart pine."

Christensen pointed out a subtle something that makes the lodge and its outdoor pavilion an irresistible spot for any sort of gathering for a member and his guests: asymmetry. Just as the logs in the building were not milled down to uniformity, he allowed no rigid spacing or repetition in the landscaping and plantings. The lack of square corners makes this an ideal spot to sit and think about birds, and golf, and the man who built this place.

Weldon Wyatt visits the lodge on occasion, and he seems to enjoy greeting friends old and new. And he likes to occasionally watch the incredible co-ordination between animals and humans in the field. But he doesn't hunt himself.

Sage Valley © Thom Abbott Golf Collection 2007

CHAPTER 7

FRIENDS

THAT I DIDN'T MARRY BRENDA FIRST.

AND THAT I DIDN'T FINISH HIGH SCHOOL OR GO TO COLLEGE.

—WELDON WYATT, DESCRIBING HIS REGRETS

*W*illiam Gregg built the textile mill in Graniteville in 1845. Mr. Gregg frowned through his beard in all the available photographs, but he must have been a kind man. Or at least a caring one: he required the children of his mill hands to attend school at least until sixth grade. Nickel-a-day fine if they didn't.

He electrified every house in town. He instituted a truancy law. He bought every student's textbooks. Weldon Wyatt knows these things and more about the founder of the Graniteville mill. He admires William Gregg, and he's nostalgic about the paternalistic society the mills created and that he grew up in.

Perhaps it's going too far to say that the shopping centers he built—hubs of commerce and employment—replicated the mills. It may also be a stretch to compare Gregg to a man seated amidst the luxury of a golf and hunt club three miles away and 150 years later. But the comparisons became unavoidable when, in 2007, Wyatt led a group that bought the defunct Graniteville mill.

The Columbia *State* headlined its page one story on the deal HANGING BY A THREAD OF HOPE. An accompanying chart entitled "South Carolina's Vanishing Textile Jobs" showed that 135,400 in the Palmetto State made a living making thread and cloth in 1990. Of the 31,000 South Carolinians in textiles today, Wyatt already employed one hundred, in a company he owns called Graniteville Specialty Fabrics. GSF makes such as waterproof fabric for golf bags.

WELDON WYATT, A 68-YEAR-OLD REAL ESTATE DEVELOPER AND SON OF MILL WORKERS, IS LEADING AN INVESTMENT GROUP THAT PLANS TO PRESERVE THE HISTORIC GRANITEVILLE, VAUCLUSE, AND WARRENVILLE MILLS, AND REUSE THEM FOR APARTMENTS, CONDOS, OFFICES, AND SHOPS.

"WE WANT TO RE-VITALIZE THE GRANITEVILLE AREA," WYATT SAID. "WE THINK IT'S GOT A GREAT FUTURE. I BELIEVE IN FIVE OR SIX YEARS GRANITEVILLE WILL BE A LOT BETTER OFF THAN IT WAS AS A TEXTILE MILL.

"I DON'T WANT GRANITEVILLE TO GO LIKE A LOT OF THE MILL VILLAGES—JUST DIE AND WITHER AWAY. I'VE BEEN HERE FIFTY YEARS. I KNOW WHAT GREAT PEOPLE THEY ARE. THEY DESERVE BETTER."

—THE COLUMBIA STATE, SEPTEMBER 3, 2007

Will his support of the mills and his particular mill valley define Weldon Wyatt's time on earth? No one can say how history or History will remember him, and Wyatt doesn't pretend to know. But he doesn't think of Sage Valley as his monument.

"The legacy of Sage Valley is not me," Wyatt says. "It's gonna be Tom. He will be the one to build this club for the next forty or fifty years. He's really the only Wyatt left. He turned out to be such a great son. And if anyone had an excuse not to be...I remember Woody [the Wyatt's valet] following him around with a cooler during those junior golf tournaments so that he wouldn't get dehydrated.

ABOUT TO BOARD THE JET TO SCOTLAND

"Even when he was little, he could not lie to you. He couldn't do it! And he still can't lie to you today. I remember when he was playing in the Brad Faxon tournament in Rhode Island when he was in college, and he had a good round going, one- or two-under par. But on seventeen he hit it in the woods, and when he holed out on eighteen, he saw that he had a different Titleist 1 than the one he started with. He gave himself the penalty.

"He called me that night and said, 'Dad, I messed up.' And I told him I was more proud of him for playing by the rules than for anything else he could have done.

"Tom loves the game the same way I do. But I'd like him to know that if he ever does away with our caddie program, I'll come back to haunt him."

He's joking, I think. Yet thoughts about the big picture were never far from Wyatt's mind in 2007, because his mother, Estoy, died in May and his father, Hayden, passed in August. The tenth anniversary of Joe's death caused some long thoughts. And while he remembered them he remembered his dear friend Jack Stephens, the former chairman of Augusta National. "What a great guy," Wyatt says. "I thought we had the same interests. He cared about people."

Stephens had been very ill after a stroke, and near the end his voice was a hoarse whisper. Wyatt paid a final visit to his home in Little Rock. Instead of hello, Stephens said, "You makin' any money?" And instead of goodbye, "I love you." He died two months later.

In 2007, Wyatt also took care to cherish the friends he could still talk to and laugh with. Particularly his company on the bus: Dr. Randy Shelley, Dr. Ronny Lee, Bob Marshall, David Poole, and Sam Phillips.

The Chinese say the way to immortality is simple: plant a tree, write a book, or have a child. Weldon Wyatt's done all three now. I don't think he'll be forgotten.

LESLIE, WELDON, ASHLEY with WYATT, BRENDA
TOM with WELLS and MARYBREN with JOHN

Acknowledgments

Primary thanks go to Weldon Wyatt, editor Jim Cruise, book designer Suzanna Brown, and Rosa Loyo.

I'm also grateful to Holly Roehrig Lee for her assistance with Wal-Mart; Peggy Hurley of the Tri-Pacolet Library; Julianne B. Arnold; and Pacolet Mayor Elaine Harris.

The staff at Sage Valley, hired for their combination of competence and friendliness, never disappointed. Kristie Pittard, the Director of Member Services, expressed the attitude best: "we don't tell people 'no' here." So, thanks: Daniel Seawell, Matt Stewart, and Austin Bell in the Golf Shop; waiters Johnny Williams, Vernon Oliver, Charlie Wright, Kalvin Tanksley and Patrick Miller; front door and transportation men Bob White, Carl Russaw, Antoine Peterson, Jay Allen, Ronald Wilson, Bob Smith, and John Maronski; Lilly Drayton and Luis Diaz in Security; and Janae Perkins and Kadi Meldrum in the office.

And to everyone who sat still for an interview, thank you for sharing.

BIBLIOGRAPHY

Augusta and Aiken in Golf's Golden Age by Stan Byrdy
Arcadia Publishing, Charleston, SC 2002

The Big Fix Inside the S & L Scandal by James Ring Adams
John Wiley and Sons Inc. New York 1990

Gastonia 1929 The Story of the Loray Mill Strike by John A Salmond
University of North Carolina Press 1995

James Henry Hammond and the Old South A Design for Mastery
by Drew Gilpin Faust
Louisiana State University Press Baton Rouge 1982

The Glory and the Dream A Narrative History of America 1932-1972
by William Manchester
Little, Brown New York 1974

Like a Family The Making of a Southern Cotton Mill World
by Jacquelyn Dowd Hall, James Leloudis, Robert Korstad, Mary Murphy, Lu Ann Jones,
and Christopher B. Daly
University of North Carolina Press 1987

Sam Walton The Inside Story of America's Richest Man by Vance H. Trimble
Dutton New York 1990

South Carolina A History by Walter Edgar
University of South Carolina Columbia 1998

These Are Our Lives by the Federal Writers' Project of the Works Progress Administration
University of North Carolina Press, Chapel Hill 1939

TRUMP The Art of the Deal by Donald J. Trump and Tony Schwartz
Warner Books 1987

About The Author

Former club and touring professional Curt Sampson has been writing full-time since November 1988. Among his previous books were *New York Times* bestsellers *Hogan* (1996) and *The Masters* (1998). Sampson's titles up to now:

Texas Golf Legends

The Eternal Summer

Full-Court Pressure

Hogan

The Masters

Royal and Ancient

Chasing Tiger

Five Fundamentals (with Steve Elkington)

The Lost Masters

The Slam

Centennial

Sampson's newest book, *Golf Dads*, will be available in March 2008. Curtsampson.com is his website; his email address is msampson@joimail.com

SAGE VALLEY PHOTOGRAPHY

Involved with graphic design since elementary school, Thom Abbott incorporates his composition skills into every photo. Best known for his Golf Course Photography, Thom has now photographed many prestigious golf courses including Sage Valley Golf Club. Thom's work has been published in many magazines including *Links, Golf Digest,* and *Stratos.*

Thom owns and operates Southside Gallery in Aiken, SC. The website address is www.southsidegallery.com.

Sage Valley © Thom Abbott Golf Collection 2007